CHERRY C

# The Disrupted Season (2019-20)

A relegation battle for Bournemouth that would go down to the last day of the season

By Peter Bell
The Blog author of Cherry Chimes

©2020 Peter Bell
All rights reserved.

ISBN: 9798682844197
First printed edition 2020.

# About the author

Peter Bell, 53, is a trade magazine commissioning editor at International Cement Review. He has written on AFC Bournemouth since 2013 when he started his *Cherry Chimes blog*.

Having written comments on AFC Bournemouth for *The Times, The Telegraph, The Guardian, The Observer, The Daily Mail* and *The Sun*, Peter has become one of the go-to contacts for information from fans on how AFC Bournemouth are performing. He has also appeared on *TalkSport* and *BBC 5 Live radio* as well as local radio stations.

Peter has a season ticket in the North Stand and likes to attend games with his two sons, Robert and Stephen Bell.

This is the second book he has written on the Cherries (AFC Bournemouth's nickname), having published *Eddie Had A Dream (1994-2019)* in October 2019. It was the logical step to continue the story with the next on AFC Bournemouth's top-flight history. While this book looks in more depth at what happened in a single season, Peter hopes that *The Disrupted Season* is something that fans will look back on as a unique time when our lives were changed beyond all recognition. Sport became unimportant in comparison to the NHS working harder than ever to save lives during the coronavirus pandemic.

# Acknowledgements

I have had some help writing this book and I must thank my family for allowing me to spend time researching and writing, when I could have been spending more time with them.

Lockdown was a challenge for everyone, but it did give me time to keep writing. I was pleased that I could call on some help for this book, from my good friend Michael Dunne, author of *Dean Court Days: Harry Redknapp's reign at Bournemouth* and owner of the All Departments podcast.

I must also thank Paul Orchard who owns the *In off The Far Post* football memorabilia shop in Pokesdown, Bournemouth. Paul was kind enough to sell my first book and encouraged me to write a second book.

By buying this book you will be helping the charity for which Eddie Howe is patron - Julia's House Children's Hospice. The author is donating 15 per cent of the earnings from this book to this local charity.

Finally, thanks to fellow fans who continue to read what I write daily on the *Cherry Chimes* blog.

# Contents

| | |
|---|---|
| About the Author | iii |
| Acknowledgements | v |
| Contents | vii |
| Why be a blogger? | ix |
| Introduction | xiii |
| Chapter 1. May – July 2019<br>*Summer preparations and pre-season* | *1* |
| Chapter 2. August 2019 –<br>*The new boys & the Champions* | *33* |
| Chapter 3. September 2019 –<br>*The Carabao Cup goes for a Burton* | *49* |
| Chapter 4. October 2019 –<br>*The goalless month* | *69* |

Chapter 5. November 2019 –
*United, they fall* — 87

Chapter 6. December 2019 –
*It's a relegation fight* — 113

Chapter 7. January 2020 –
*Down but not out* — 133

Chapter 8. February 2020 –
*In the Mire* — 157

Chapter 9. March 2020 –
*Coronavirus* — 179

Chapter 10 April 2020 –
*Lockdown* — 201

Chapter 11 May 2020 –
*Project Restart* — 211

Chapter 12 June 2020 –
*Football returns* — 225

Chapter 13 July 2020 –
*No way back?* — 237

Chapter 14
*Player index* — 275

# Why be a blogger?

Why indeed be a blogger? Following a football team is hard enough in itself. The anguish and heartfelt disappointments and the fleeting moments of jubilation never seem enough for some fans. Writing about your team is a way to let go of some of the passion and feelings that build up. I'm one of those people who needs to share a view, just to get it off my chest. Watching football is a community thing. We like to get other peoples' opinions and see how close, or far away they are from our own opinions.

Don't get me wrong. There are some negatives about being a blogger or a podcaster. People don't always like what you say, and opposition comments can be hurtful or damn right nasty. I tend to filter out those that are just not suitable for publishing on the blog. But why some fans choose to be so aggressive to other fans that, just like them, look forward to watching a game, I find it hard to fathom. The football family is the way I like to think about the game. There have been many remarkable tales of fans from one club respecting the fans of another club, and helping them out when misfortune struck.

By writing a daily blog you soon realise that you are only touching the surface of what is probably happening at your club. Some things will never be written down or spoken of, but the thoughts of fans are some of the most intriguing aspects of following the game. It's a section of history that has never really been seen as important enough to document when the cups are handed out but, without the fans, the game isn't really the same which would become all too clear in 2019-20.

I hope that in years to come, some football fans pick up books like this and realise that they too can write about their club and engage with fellow fans. If we don't write anything down, then those memories may well disappear. Yet, they are what encourage people to go to games every week. If you have supporters that have been going to games for 20, 30, or 40 years or more, they are the special fans that should be cherished by all at a club. Their memories can re-live in detail some of the epic moments in games that have happened in a club's history. I have no doubt when you hear them first hand, they are much more vivid than when reading them from a book.

But still, a book, podcast, vlog, or a blog is a valuable resource for remembering what happened in the past. There are parts of games that we forget, humorous moments, woeful attempts at goal and wonderful saves. It is hard for us to separate all the games, and after, a while, it becomes hard to separate the seasons. At least I find it hard to remember sometimes, perhaps it's my age?

When I wrote *Eddie Had A Dream*, I soon found that it was much harder to get things correct than I had imagined. Dates, scores, names, positions, transfers and substitutions are just the tip of the iceberg. I didn't get everything right and I hope to do better this time, just as we hope our players improve every season.

Just like on the field, nobody wants to make mistakes. A pen is a powerful tool though, as it stays written and there is a responsibility to try and get as close to the truth as possible. But when you read this book, I also hope that you can enjoy the sense of remembering some of the games and perhaps you'll recall the things that are special to you, like sitting next to a certain fan and reliving that moment when you celebrated a goal or applauded for a terrific save.

These moments or memories are something to be treasured. If I can put a few more smiles on the faces of fans that had forgotten something that happened during the disrupted season, then I'll be happy to have achieved what I set out to do.

UTCIAD! (Up The Cherries, In All Departments)

# Introduction

You would think that after learning that it was a difficult task to write about football that I might have learned my lesson. I clearly haven't! After the reviews of many AFC Bournemouth fans and the success of my first publication – *Eddie Had A Dream* – I am back on my laptop and punching out a few more words on the keyboard about our beloved Cherries.

Luckily, I don't have to write about 25-years this time. I have the narrower time-frame in mind of AFC Bournemouth's fifth season in the Premier League 2019-20. It makes sense, of course, following on from where the last book left off. So, if you haven't read *Eddie Had A Dream* yet, what are you doing here?

I found that I could draw upon what Cherry Chimes has had to say over the past season, to get as close to the action as possible. You will see some familiar match reports, but with additional thoughts here and there and some reflection on what has passed. I didn't expect it to be such a dramatic season, but it is a season that will probably live with us for many years. Following AFC Bournemouth battling with relegation, while the coronavirus pandemic threatened the completion of the whole season, was an incredible experience. Nobody could have foreseen a world of social distancing and staying at home when the first ball was kicked in August 2019.

I never quite know how a season is going to work out. In the summer months, before all the action has begun, like most of you, I try and give a prediction of how it might go. I often have to do this anyway, as other blog writers, or newspapers, will try and get it out of me however they can. At the end of the season, you always feel a bit of a fool, when you see your predictions being so far out. For 2019-20, I plumped for the league title going to Liverpool, after their near-miss in the previous season. The rest of the top four I thought would be made up of Man City second, Tottenham Hotspur third and Arsenal fourth.

My thoughts on who would suffer the humiliation of being relegated from the Premier League was much harder to decide. I was worried that we could lose one of our south coast derbies, and I slipped Brighton & Hove Albion into the bottom three in 18$^{th}$ place. The Seagulls did have a bit of a wobble in 2018-19 and had parted company with Chris Hughton, who I felt was a steady pair of hands. I had no idea who Graham Potter was, or how he might fair for the first time in the Premier League. Having seen newly-promoted Fulham get it all wrong the previous season, I predicted the other promoted sides in 2018-

19 to be under a lot of pressure. For that reason, I picked Sheffield United to finish 19th and the bottom vacancy to be filled by Aston Villa.

We will see how I did later. Oh, I thought you wouldn't ask. Where did I place the Cherries? While I was optimistic Eddie Howe's squad might be a bit stronger than the previous season, I didn't go overboard and picked a safe but solid 12th place for AFC Bournemouth.

Getting off to a good start is what every fan wants for their team. While I doubted Bournemouth would get 20 points from their first 10 games, as they did in 2018-19, I had high expectations when I saw the fixture list. I was hopeful that AFC Bournemouth could be in the upper echelons of the table early on. Playing Sheffield United and Aston Villa first up was not a bad draw by the Premier League's fixture computer, even if someone was having a laugh when they threw in Man City for the third game – just to stop us being top of the league, I imagined. But no season plays out as you expect. Several of AFC Bournemouth's players were not even expected to be fit until well into October and November. Thinking about the start of the season as the first game drew near, I began to panic a little before a ball was even kicked.

# Chapter 1.
# Summer preparations

I always use the pre-season friendlies as an early indicator of what the season ahead might bring. I don't know why, because the games are always against clubs that your team won't be playing in the league. Still, you have to get a form guide from somewhere.

    We'd have to wait a little while to find out who AFC Bournemouth were lining up to play when the curtain came down on the 2018-19 season. Bournemouth had finished in 14th place having lost out in a 5-3 goal-busting match at Selhurst Park in the last game of the season. The Cherries made a slow start and were 3-1 down at half-time with Jefferson Lerma hitting a thunderbolt of a goal that would win him the Cherries' goal of the season. You could say he left it late to score such a blinding goal from 30 yards out and straight in the top corner, but Jefferson had been one of the stars of 2018-19 for AFC Bournemouth. Jordon Ibe had not had such a fabulous season, but he did get on the score sheet in this game. Bournemouth had looked like they might make a fight of it in the second half, having clawed it back to 3-2. But Crystal Palace would take all three points and the 11th spot in the final table, when Patrick van Aanholt and Andros Townsend brought a close to Bournemouth's 2018-19 season with a young Mark Travers wondering what had just happened, following his clean sheet against Tottenham Hotspur on debut the previous weekend.

Bournemouth ended their fourth Premier League season, having fallen just a point short of their record 46 point total from 2016-17. Still, the Cherries had again finished above Southampton, as well as Brighton & Hove Albion, to confirm they were now the best team in the south.

No sooner had the season finished than AFC Bournemouth went straight into the transfer market to buy Lloyd Kelly, 20, of Bristol City for a reported £13m. Speaking on the club website, Eddie Howe revealed that Kelly was a key acquisition for the club. 'Lloyd is an exciting talent and a player of real potential, while at the same time already possessing good experience for someone so young,' said the Bournemouth manager.

On *Cherry Chimes*, I had some thoughts on the new signing. 'Kelly will give new competition to AFCB's problem position of left-back. While Kelly has only made 48 appearances in all competitions for Bristol City over the last two seasons, he has impressed Bournemouth's scouting team. The defender joined Bristol City form the age of 12 and is a product of the Bristol City Academy.

Lloyd only made his first team debut for Bristol City in a Carabao Cup match against Plymouth in 2017. He has since scored twice in the Championship and was awarded Championship Player of the week on 19 March 2018, for week 38 of the 2017-18 season.' It all sounded very impressive. Eddie Howe was bringing in recruits who could improve on the defence which had let in a staggering 70 goals in 2018-19, a total which was only better than two of the relegated sides, Fulham and Huddersfield, who had conceded 81 and 76 goals, respectively.

But it wasn't just the left-back position that was being looked at. The goalkeeping position also seemed up for grabs. Mark Travers had come in and played the last two matches of the 2018-19 season, and it seemed that Asmir Begović was now surplus to requirements. Yet, as the summer progressed there was no end of talk and speculation about who Bournemouth should sign to play between the sticks. While Jack Butland had been the front runner for some time, it wasn't clear that Stoke City were keen on letting him go at a bargain price. I was keen to know where Bournemouth would look for their next keeper, just as much as any other fan, and on 23 May 2018 I picked up on the gossip that Nick Pope was suddenly in the frame.

# THE DISRUPTED SEASON (2019-20)

'While Pope had a great season at Burnley the season before last, he has been unable to get a game in the most recent Premier League season and we don't know what his form is like at the moment. It does kind of nark me that when it comes to picking keepers, AFCB tends to look at options that other clubs are very willing to palm off if you'll forgive the hand pun.

Burnley is indeed overstocked with Englishmen vying for the national keeper's shirt, let alone their club No 1 spot, but there are surely more options than just England keepers to pick from. Oh, and don't we want a keeper who is in form? Foreign keepers dominate the Premier League and none of the top six clubs have an English keeper. It is a bit different though further down the league. Everton has Jordan Pickford, Watford Ben Foster and, of course, Burnley has Joe Hart and Tom Heaton, while Palace has Welshman Wayne Hennessey. However, the days of British keepers being at the top of the game have arguably been surpassed.'

Okay, I might have been a bit over the top in feeling that the British keeper was a dying breed. But how many of us would think that Eddie Howe would enjoy the competition between the four keepers he already had at the club vying for the number one shirt? The prize would be kept a secret right up until the last minute. We didn't know if it would be Artur Boruc, Asmir Begović, Aaron Ramsdale or Mark

Travers who would be picked to start. But Mark Travers looked in pole position having played in the last two Premier League games.

Concerns among the fans were also being raised in another area of the field. Ryan Fraser had admitted in interviews that he had not signed a new contract at Bournemouth and had just a year left on his deal. Arsenal were prime movers to sign the 'Wee-man', as we affectionately called him. I was fairly relaxed about the position, as Ryan had been excellent for the club and deserved a move if he wanted it. As always, I had something to say as always on *Cherry Chimes*.

'Always his harshest critic, Fraser says he will go away and look at his season and what he could do better himself. Fraser has developed with the Howe philosophy of working hard on your game to improve. The worry for AFCB fans is that Fraser may feel that some other players who have been at AFCB, at least as long as him, have not managed to turn potential into becoming developed, confident and exceptional players.'

If Bournemouth had a team of players that wanted to be as good as Ryan Fraser, the team would be in a much better place. But Fraser is dedicated to getting better, and he could not have done much more, in my opinion, in 2018-19. I felt he would look at what AFCB's plans are for the new season and decide, based on that and what he could do elsewhere.

I concluded that 'Ryan says everything that is happening is good. He is in a good place if you like. He wins either way, whether he stays or goes. But AFCB can't have player power driving Dean Court and they must take precautions in case the Wee-man does take flight this summer.'

One player that looked more certain to make a transfer out of Dean Court was Tyrone Mings. Tyrone had, as usual, had a season that was interrupted with injuries and he perhaps needed to try his luck elsewhere. That was expected to be at Aston Villa as Mings had spent the previous four months there on loan. Before he could decide, he had a big match to play in, but not for AFCB as I mentioned on *Cherry Chimes*.

'This coming Bank Holiday Monday, Tyrone Mings is expected to be a central figure in trying to get Aston Villa to the Premier League in the Championship play-off final with Derby Country. Tyrone has been at Aston Villa since January, since when their up-turn in form has pushed them towards their tilt at Premier League football. But what will happen after the match if Aston Villa wins promotion?'

I had my thoughts on that, too. 'Whether it was in AFCB's mind to get him out on loan to try and get him to move club is not so clear. But Tyrone has never had a successful run of games in the side, starting just 11 matches for AFCB. While he has been excellent when he has played, the injuries have held his AFCB career back. It could be a point in time where AFCB decides they can recoup some money for him, by letting him move on.'

I was treading rather well on AFC Bournemouth's transfer plans it seemed, even if I didn't necessarily know it. The 28 May 2019 saw me post a story on whether Liverpool's Harry Wilson could be joining the Cherries.

'With the play-off final between Derby and Aston Villa taking place yesterday,' I said,' there was a great opportunity to see the work of Liverpool's Harry Wilson who is on loan at Derby. *The Sun* has been clear that AFCB is among the front-runners to gain the right-winger's signature, if Derby slipped up against Villa as they did, although Wolves, Crystal Palace and Brighton are also keen on the 22-year-old.

'A sticking point for fans and AFCB is that Harry Wilson is reported to cost in the region of £25m as Liverpool look to cash in on their youngster. AFCB may only make three or four signings, and it does seem a big fee for a player that has only played one game in the Premier League, even if he is a full Welsh international. The 18 goals he has scored in the Championship are a good indication that he has the talent to step up.'

*The Sun's* information was good, but we didn't

know that at the time, and we'd have to wait and see if more Welsh youngsters would arrive at Dean Court. What we could assume is that Liverpool is usually a good source for new signings. Many of the fans wanted one Liverpool defender, in particular, to sign permanently. Yes, Nathaniel Clyne is the man I'm talking about and, having signed on loan at the start of the year, there was every hope that a permanent deal could be done. Rather like Brexit though, nothing seemed to be happening.

I penned this on 27 May 2019. 'AFCB have been reported to be making enquiries about the availability of Nathaniel Clyne from Liverpool, after a successful loan period on the south coast. For me, Clyne is the perfect player to keep making AFCB progress. He is an international who has been with one of the top six clubs and he works hard at his game.

'The right-back position could well be Nathaniel's next season if he does sign on a permanent deal. While Simon Francis will be making his comeback and Adam Smith is often seen as the utility man, Clyne has a great chance of having a starting spot and perhaps vying to get his England place back.'

Unfortunately, it was not to be but there was interest in another Liverpool man for a short while. *'The Sun* claims that their latest target is Liverpool's Simon Mignolet, who has made just two appearances for Liverpool this past season. Mignolet has plenty of experience, but the price is expected to be in the region of £15m, and it is anyone's guess whether Mignolet can find his best form again.'

I wasn't sure that Bournemouth was the best place for him. 'Mignolet's value is where AFCB might struggle to see Liverpool's point of view on him. AFCB has never paid more than £10m for a keeper and, if they are to jump up to £15m, there are probably other candidates that also come into the mix.'

While the transfer market trundled on with few signings being made by mid-June, I started to get more distracted by what was happening in the international arena of football. Callum Wilson was being picked regularly now for England, so Bournemouth fans were keen to see England play. One aspect of the game that we knew was going to change for the upcoming season was the introduction of Video Assistant Referee (VAR). Just to sharpen our thoughts on what a different season it could be with VAR, Callum was caught out with VAR in the Nation's League Third-place play-off match for England against Switzerland.

'We had to wait a long time for Gareth Southgate to finally give Callum Wilson his third run out for England, but he did get on towards the end of the second half against Switzerland in the Nation's League Third Place play-off. It was a game where I would have thought Southgate would play a few of the players on the fringe of the starting 11, but he played a pretty strong team, and England only narrowly squeaked through on penalties after extra-time.

The talking point of the game though was Callum Wilson's disallowed goal. Raheem Sterling had made made a good cross from the left byline that reached Dele Alli. Alli's header came off the crossbar, which Wilson quickly pounced upon to stab into the goal. The finish was a typical Wilson poacher's goal, and at first, few people could see anything wrong with the goal, which was celebrated by England fans.

'However, VAR was activated and the referee took a close look at the build-up in which it could be seen that Wilson pulled back his defender, before making his way towards the six-yard box. Without VAR I don't expect that it would have been picked up, and we are going to have to get used to this kind of thing next season. Wilson too is going to have to see that he won't get away with it if he tries this kind of thing in the future.'

While one Bournemouth international was getting his first taste of tournament football, Nathan Aké was in the news, as he was being courted by Tottenham Hotspur. I was far from happy about it. 'Reports this week in the national press that Aké is being targeted by Tottenham are no surprise. Bournemouth might consider a sum of around £40m – good business in any other area of the field – but when our team is struggling to keep the goals out, the last thing Eddie Howe will want is to sell his leading defender.

Nathan Aké might not have had his best season in 2018-19, but he had been ever-present in Bournemouth's defence. If he had not been available for so many matches, it could have been a much worse season for the Cherries. I have no doubt that Aké could play for a top-six team like Spurs and he would do a very good job, but how do you put a price on a player that you want to be at the heart of your side for the next five or more years?

'Considered in that timescale, I'd say £40m doesn't come anywhere near Aké's true value to AFCB and I'd be shocked if Bournemouth wasted anytime in considering such a bid for one of their star players.'

A popular post on the blog on 17 June was headline, 'Joe Hart – please Eddie, don't go there!' I was dumbfounded why AFC Bournemouth could even be considering a player who we knew just couldn't play out well from the back. 'What is it with AFCB always choosing the cheap option for one of the most important positions on the field? Goalkeepers are specialists and we have seen in the four years that AFCB has been in the Premier League that keepers can save a club a lot of points, while they can also be very costly. Although AFCB is being linked with former England number ones, I pondered whether they had forgotten their philosophy of playing from the back, if they do put in a bid for Joe Hart?

While the focus of the goalkeeping saga would move on to another Burnley keeper, in the shape of Tom Heaton, a few days later, I was still unconvinced that Bournemouth would make a keeper signing. On the blog, I wrote, 'Bournemouth's odds of signing Tom Heaton have come into 2-1 since the keeper decided not to extend his contract at Burnley. The Cherries have been looking for a keeper all summer, as Asmir Begović is expected to be sent on his way. But is Heaton the best option for the Cherries, seeing that they have been checking out just about every available keeper?'

Another new hurdle for the coming season, apart from VAR, would be the introduction of a winter break. February was about to be reworked without much football. Would Bournemouth benefit from it? I ran a headline on 24 June that screamed 'AFCB, already looking forward to winter break'.

'Eddie Howe has come out, commenting that he will be one manager who is grateful for the winter break in February. While the English Premier League will be trying this for the first time, we have yet to see what impact the break will have with some clubs not having a game on 8 February and others on 15 February. I'm all for the break, but feel that a two-weeks stop for all clubs at one time would have been more beneficial.'

As pessimistic as ever, I had looked closely at who the Cherries would be playing in the affected week and was perhaps more sympathetic to the break when I saw who it would be. 'Eddie Howe will take his team to Sheffield United on one of the weekends in February, on either side of the break, and it will be a key game you'd expect in trying to ensure AFCB is not engaged in a relegation battle. The game will be a tough one I'm sure, and so the break would be a big help at that time, if the game comes on 15 February.

'AFCB suffered more than their fair share of injuries last season. Anything to help reduce players' missing games must be applauded. But with just a week to relax and keep fit, rather than play games, will it have the big impact the league and the managers hope for recharging their players' batteries? Or will it have little impact?

Just as we were feeling a bit cold considering what those winter months would be like, a headline came that started to send more shivers down Bournemouth fans' spines, 'Howe among leading candidates for Newcastle job!'

Newcastle United had already taken Matt Ritchie from Bournemouth at the end of the Cherries' first season in the Premier League. We were having none of this talk of Eddie Howe driving up to the Angel of the North.

'It was a bad day for Newcastle United fans yesterday as Rafa Benítez's reign at the club came to an end. But now it will probably be bad news for another club, as Mike Ashley looks to grab a proven manager in the Premier League. While Garry Monk and Jose Mourinho are the leading contenders, *Bet888* made Eddie Howe a 9-1 shot for the vacant position, while *the BBC* had Howe as the second favourite in the first few hours after the announcement that Benítez was leaving.'

I was shocked that Howe was so high up in the running for the job, but calmed myself by looking at the bigger picture of where AFC Bournemouth was at, in its development. Put this against what anyone would inherit at the Toon, and I felt reasonably confident that a big move up north was perhaps not on the cards for Eddie Howe and Jason Tindall.

'There will come a time when Howe does look at a new challenge. We may or may not like that when it comes, and even now some might consider that Howe is keeping AFCB afloat in the Premier League, but hasn't managed to build the club into a consistent top 10 side. If that is a success for AFCB, then Howe is on the verge of repeating a top 10 finish, but staying there is not easy. What he does have is the backing of the board and owner at AFCB, which is half the battle for a manager.

Meanwhile, the summer was moving on quickly and preparations would mean departures as well as incoming players. We had already seen an old favourite in Marc Pugh call an end to his Bournemouth career after nine years and 312 appearances.

Now we had to reconcile ourselves with a player leaving who we'd hardly seen. I had to write on 27 June 2019 that 'It looks like Connor Mahoney's time at AFCB could be up. Mind you, he has been out on loan at Barnsley and Birmingham City more than he has played for AFCB, since his signing two years ago from Blackburn Rovers.

'How did we get here? My feeling is that Connor was less than pleased with being an AFCB player. He had been sent out on loan without getting an opportunity to play football for the Premier League club he signed for. Why should he see games going by without being a part of the club he wanted to be at? I kind of get this point of view. He had such a good season at Birmingham City that he knows he can rip it up in the Championship and could help a team get into the promotion places.

'Millwall's gain could be AFCB's loss though. I don't think we know how good Mahoney could become and he is still learning. The sad thing, if he does leave, is that it might not leave such a good impression with other young players who have thought about joining AFCB. While some players have thrived under Eddie Howe, others have just not been seen enough, and whether that is AFCB not taking any risks, or some players not dedicating themselves enough to the cause is a shame either way.'

I suppose it proved that not every signing can be successful for your team. In the Premier League you have to move on quickly, as the pace won't slow down with other teams buying better players all the time. Yet, Bournemouth knew who they wanted to buy and who they wanted to keep hold of.

On 8 July 2019, a new arrival walked through the doors at Dean Court. Right-back Jack Stacey, 23, had signed from Luton Town after a promotion-winning season. While several clubs had shown an interest in Jack, he knew where he wanted to go. 'This is a great club with a fantastic manager who helps establish young players, so that made it an easy decision in the end' Stacey told *AFCBTV*. 'I believe I can thrive here and can't wait to start.'

If Jack's enthusiasm could be grabbed and bottled then AFC Bournemouth would be in good shape. The need to get some young players was very evident. Eddie Howe had said at the start of the summer that this would be one of the most important windows for the club because the club needed to bring down the average age of the squad.

Keeping the much talked about Callum Wilson was a challenge of another kind. West Ham United was a likely predator. Their strategy was to go and try and get a player who had always caused them a real problem. But if the Hammers were going to chase Callum Wilson, AFC Bournemouth would make it difficult for the London club to make a raid.

'The transfer market is just ramping up and having heard that Marko Arnautović has left West

Ham for China, attention will soon turn to the Irons making a bid for Callum Wilson, I wrote at the time, 'Pellegrini is a big admirer of AFCB's number 13, probably because Wilson always scores against West Ham, and he is an England striker that would add a bit of glamour to a West Ham signing.

'I can see the interest from West Ham, but are AFCB now a big enough club to hold off the likes of West Ham when they are desperate to sign one of the Cherries' players? We haven't seen this situation before, and it will be a test of AFCB's resolve to keep one of their star players. Losing Wilson would be a big hole to fill. The stature of Wilson has been growing to such an extent that it is hard to imagine another player leading the line for the Cherries.'

There seemed little chance of West Ham succeeding though when, on 11 July, Bournemouth announced it had the finances to keep its striker. 'Callum Wilson looks set to be signing a new contract this summer with AFCB, which will be a blow to the likes of West Ham and Chelsea. *The Sun* reported that Bournemouth's number 13 is about to be given a new five-year deal worth £26m to stay on the south coast.'

Game over West Ham! Just a couple of days later Callum signed a new contract to keep himself at Bournemouth until 2023.

While Callum Wilson was extending his Bournemouth career, Aaron Ramsdale was trying to make his way into the first team. He had a fabulous game to look forward to in pre-season, as he would be facing old teammates at AFC Wimbledon, where he had been on loan in 2018-19. Aaron did indeed get to start the game against AFC Wimbledon and he made an early impression. 'It was the Callum Wilson show first half with two well-crafted goals for the Bournemouth striker, the second being truly magnificent as he lobbed the keeper. Ramsdale also made a good save in the first half to keep the clean sheet. A second half change of team brought fresh legs to the game. But Bournemouth started to make mistakes. Dan Gosling gave away a penalty and then a handball gave Wimbledon the chance to make it 2-2 from the spot, which they did. It was left to Ryan Fraser to get the Cherries out of their predicament against a Wimbledon side that were stronger in the second half. Supremacy regained, there were not so many scares as the game ran out a 3-2 win to the Cherries.

On the subject of closure, Lys Mousset called time on his AFC Bournemouth career at this point. The French striker agreed to join Sheffield United on 18 July for a reported £10m. I was surprised by the move. 'The Frenchman has found it hard to get playing time at AFCB, but it must be a gamble for Sheffield United to hope that Lys can become a big star for them in the Premier League.

'For the Cherries, Mousset is another young

player that Eddie Howe and his coaches have worked hard to try and improve. The transfer fee seems reasonable for Mousset and what he has achieved so far, and the extra money that AFCB are starting to accumulate is starting to look like some good business depending on what they do with it,' I said.

'It wouldn't surprise me if Mousset did well at Sheffield United and we saw a player that we haven't seen at AFCB. He has an incentive to do well. A fresh start at a club that has the main aim of staying up, and if he can score goals, he'll soon become a hero.'

Nothing was clear on the goalkeeping position, even if Mark Travers signed a new contract to extend his stay at AFC Bournemouth until 2022. I was just pleased that the youngsters were getting a chance. The way that Aaron Ramsdale and Mark Travers have been mixing with the first team in La Manga was great to see, but they needed to feature in the pre-season games if they were going to challenge Boruc and Begović. 'The outfield players and especially the back four need to be comfortable with whoever is going to be between the sticks, and they need to work as a unit. It's Boruc's shirt to lose I'd say, but a lot could happen in the few weeks between now and the start of the season.'

Mark Travers was in goal for the first half against Girona FC in Barcelona. The match was played on 20 July and Mark Travers did himself no harm by keeping a clean sheet in the first half. But he did have one shock when Travers hit the ball against Nathan Aké and almost saw the ball go into AFCB's net on 17 minutes. 'Bournemouth offered stiff resistance to a Girona FC side that had the advantage of 11 men against 10 for much of the second half. Jack Simpson was the unlucky man to be sent off for a foul on Marc Gual when he was the last man. When Gual put the Catalans ahead with 10 minutes to go, it looked all over, but Ryan Fraser popped up with an equaliser a minute later. The lifeline was short-lived though, as Girona scored again with Juanpe's header from a corner five minutes from time.'

The team flew home just in time to play a 0-0 draw away at WBA on 26 July. Aaron Ramsdale was the player that everyone was talking about after the game. 'It was the saves of Aaron Ramsdale and the work of the midfield that impressed against WBA,' I reported.

Summing up the match against the Baggies I said, 'A good exercise for the Cherries and a clean sheet. Eddie Howe will be pleased that the team didn't run out of steam, but he'll have Aaron Ramsdale to thank the most for the score line. The strikers have to do a bit more in front of goal, but the shape of the team when defending was a bit stronger in this game with Harry Arter and Nnamdi Ofoborh offering good protection.'

The friendly against Brentford FC at Griffin Park on 27 July was a chance for players like Jordon Ibe, David

# SUMMER PREPARATIONS 21

Brooks and Dominic Solanke to get their pre-season scoring going. We were not disappointed. 'The Cherries had a good spread of first team players out against Brentford and Jordon Ibe, Dominic Solanke and Sam Surridge got the goals for Bournemouth at a rain-soaked Griffin Park. The Cherries had to defend at times and made the most of Brentford making a few mistakes. Still, Brentford did get one goal back, by substitute Marcus Forss, in the last five minutes.'

The big concern was that David Brooks had come off injured after damaging his ankle. We were right to be concerned, as he would miss the start of the season. The most amusing part of the afternoon was listening to Steve Fletcher sharing the match commentary. He was adamant that the ball would be a Championship ball in the first half and a Premier League ball in the second half, as he had arranged it with Brentford. It would give Bournemouth's players a chance to get used to the ball that they would use in the Premier League. So, imagine Steve's disbelief when the Championship ball that was used in the first half and came out again for the second half. Steve's reaction – well, it was priceless. Let's just say, he was not amused!

Bournemouth's team for the Brentford match was as follows:

**AFCB**
42 Travers, 17 Stacey, 33 Mepham, 36 Butcher

(Cordner 77), 5 Aké (C), 21 Rico, 8 Lerma
(Anthony 75), 53 Kilkenny (Sherring 85), 10 Ibe,
20 Brooks (Surridge 71), 9 Solanke

**AFCB Subs**
40 Dennis, 25 Cordner, 38 Sherring, 29 Anthony, 44 Surridge

While Bournemouth was doing well on the pitch there was still a lot of disquiet about what would happen to one or two players who were expected to leave. The central midfield area was going to see some disruption, as Bournemouth signed Philip Billing from Huddersfield Town. I was happy to see a player with Premier League experience joining the squad, even if I didn't know who would miss out.

'Howe of course wants competition for places and to improve the team and with Nathan Aké having to play in central midfield at times last season, it looked clear that the squad was perhaps a player short in this department, with the long-term injury to Lewis Cook. I like the idea of having a tall central midfield player for the Cherries, and Billing is said to be a very mobile player that has great running power. If his passing and tackling is also top quality, it could be a major signing.'

My next post concerned one player who could now leave – Harry Arter. But where would he end up? My punt was to guess it would be Fulham. 'With the signing of Philip Billing looking to be over the line, attention has turned to Harry Arter and the possibility of him heading off to Fulham to join brother-in-law Scott Parker on loan. Harry has played in the full pre-season for AFCB, but with another central midfielder coming to Dean Court, it is clear that Arter sees his future elsewhere, and with Fulham being a London club, it works out well for him and his family who have been living in London over the last year.

'Playing with the number 88 shirt this season was one thing that brought a smile to fans' faces this summer. Arter loves his number eight, which he had at AFCB for many seasons before Jefferson Lerma took it last summer. The midfielder might get it back at a new club, but played with the number seven shirt at Cardiff the previous year.'

Harry would go to Fulham on loan, but we'd have to wait to see it much later in the window.

Come the 1 August, I was concerned with the number of injuries that the club now had just a couple of weeks before the start of the new campaign. 'According to a report in the *Bournemouth Echo*, the Cherries have been hit with another two injuries before the start of the season. David Brooks had suffered ankle damage from the match against Brentford when he was subbed on 71 minutes, and Lloyd Kelly is said to be out after suffering ankle ligament damage in training. Where does this leave AFCB?'

## THE DISRUPTED SEASON (2019-20)

The injuries were one thing, but the mess they made of preparations was another. I hoped that Eddie could come up with a plan to fill the holes. He needed to because David Brooks was likely to undergo surgery which would keep him out for more than two months, while Kelly was expected to be out for a shorter period, but would be sure to miss the games in August and September. Charlie Daniels was coming back to fitness, along with Simon Francis, Lewis Cook and Adam Smith, but it would be a while before we saw any of them.

Speculation in the transfer market was bubbling nicely with the *Bournemouth Echo* claiming that AFCB were closing in on the signing of Dutchman Arnaut Danjuma of Club Brugge, rated at £13.7m, *and The Sun* claiming AFCB were preparing a £25m bid for Liverpool's Harry Wilson. They were both right.

Arnaut Danjuma signed on 1 August 2019 from Club Bruges and was the fourth signing of the summer after Lloyd Kelly, Jack Stacey and Philip Billing. The numbers for AFCB's squad were starting to swell again.

Arnaut Danjuma gave a special interview to *AFCBTV* viewers. 'Coming to AFC Bournemouth is a really good step up for me," Danjuma told his new fans. "The Premier League is a great place to play your football, especially at a club like this.

'I'm excited to be here. The last 24 hours have

# SUMMER PREPARATIONS 25

been a bit crazy, but I'm delighted to be at the club and I've only heard positive things about it.

'I think the way the team plays suits my style, I like to attack and I cannot wait to get started.'

At least Eddie Howe had more than enough players to play two big international friendlies against Lazio and Champions League qualifiers Olympic Lyons. The first game against Lazio turned out to be a seven-goal thriller. Here was my quick opening summary of the game at Dean Court.

'The game started in a fairly relaxing manner. Lazio took a lead with a quick move up the left side, after a corner, and Travers was disappointed not to make the save. Jefferson Lerma levelled things up with a well taken shot from the edge of the box before Solanke stole in to make it 2-1, before half-time. While VAR was tested with a Lazio goal ruled out, Bournemouth had shown some encouraging moments. Yet, within 10 minutes of the restart, AFCB were 2-3 down, after goals from Alberto and Parolo. Correa then made it 2-4 with 15 minutes to go. Jack Stacey pulled back a consolation goal with eight minutes to go, but Bournemouth had been beaten.'

I was impressed with Bournemouth going forward, but there were obvious areas to improve on. 'A tough game for the Cherries,' I summarised. 'Bournemouth found it difficult to dominate despite being ahead at half-time, and Lazio were excellent in front of goal. Bournemouth perhaps gave possession away a bit too easily at times, but it was good to see Charlie Daniels get some 70 minutes and Andrew Surman showing he had plenty of energy. But the goal for Jack Stacey will also give him a bit of pleasure on his home debut. AFCB will have to do more work on trying to get nearer to obtaining clean sheets. This has to be Howe's major concern heading into the new season, along with the injuries the team has been picking up – hopefully, all came through the game okay in this one.'

The Lazio game line up for Bournemouth on 2 August was as follows:

**AFCB**
42 Travers (Begović 45), 33 Mepham, 36 Butcher (Surridge 76), 25 Simpson, 17 Stacey, 8 Lerma, 6 Surman (Dobre 66), 11 Daniels (Jordan), 10 Ibe, 24 Fraser, 9 Solanke

**AFCB Subs**
27 Begović, 40 Dennis, 55 Jordan, 38 Sherring, 29 Zemura, 24 Ofoborh, 54 Dobre, 44 Surridge

As if we had been short of games, another one came around straight away on 3 August with Olympic Lyons taking on the Cherries at Dean Court. The match was a surprisingly comfortable 3-0 win for the Cherries and it was great to finally see a clean sheet.

# SUMMER PREPARATIONS

My headline ran 'Kilkenny stars in AFCB's 3-0 win over Lyons'.

'While Olympic Lyons threatened early on, it was Bournemouth that looked ready for European football. Once the Cherries had taken the lead with Callum Wilson netting, they never looked back. A second goal from young winger Gavin Kilkenny rounded-off for him what would be a man of the match display. The second half didn't see Artur Buroc make as many saves as Aaron Ramsdale and Josh King made sure of a Bournemouth win, slotting home the third goal with 18 minutes to go,' said *Cherry Chimes*.

It was easy to be pleased with the performance and the result. Eddie Howe must have felt reassured that despite the injuries the team was starting to get on the right track. This is how I reviewed the game, 'A great result for Bournemouth. The clean sheet is very timely going into the start of the new season and neither Ramsdale nor Boruc looked under pressure very often. The real surprise was Gavin Kilkenny, who lit up the first half with his fast breakaways on the right and his good vision. Billing and Danjuma fitted in well and Ofoborh was very involved, while King and Callum Wilson looked much more tuned in for this game. Steve Cook came through 66 minutes as well, so a good day all round for Bournemouth.'

Here is the match line-up for the Olympic Lyons match.

**AFCB**
Ramsdale, A Smith (Zamoura 76), S Cook (Dobre 66), Aké, Rico, Kilkenny, Billing (Jordan 60), Ofoborh, Danjuma, Wilson (Surridge 76), King (Sam Sherring 86)

**AFCB**
Boruc, Dennis, Corey Jordan, Jordan Zemura, Surridge, Dobre, Sam Sherring

The match against Olympic Lyons was of most importance for Steve Cook. He'd returned for his first game and it went pretty much according to plan. It was great to see a leader back on the pitch. 'Steve Cook finally got a run out after his long-term groin injury on Saturday. To see him line up next to Nathan Aké again will have given a lot of pleasure to Eddie Howe, who is still waiting for Simon Francis to recover from his cruciate ligament injury. The importance of Cook is not just that he is so familiar with being paired with Nathan Aké at centre-back, but the fact that he is a leader and the captain on the pitch while Francis is unavailable.'

However, I was not entirely reassured that the return of Steve Cook would necessarily mean that the clean sheets would start to come. 'The thing that fans should be asking though is whether Bournemouth will concede fewer goals than last season? If the central two defenders are lining up again for the new season, can we expect them to be better because they have another season behind them? Was it the central defender's mistakes that led to most of the goals against AFCB last season? Eddie Howe looks to be satisfied that he can rely on Steve Cook to be the best partner for Aké. While Chris Mepham will surely play some games and will provide competition, it's Steve Cook that Eddie has always wanted to keep hold of. Being one of the consistent factors in Bournemouth's success, it is hard for Howe to change his view. Perhaps he feels that it is in other areas where the goals need to be stopped?

'The match against Lyons gave us a good opportunity to see what Philip Billing could do. He spread the ball very well to the wide areas and was not afraid to play the odd long ball, which was accurate and put Bournemouth on the front foot. He did find himself chasing back on the wrong side a couple of times against Lyons' quick breaks, but it was a solid enough performance for a player that hadn't been with the squad more than a couple of days.'

With the first league match against Sheffield United, it was the right time to ask who would start in central midfield? Philip Billing was now getting game time, while Jefferson Lerma and Andrew Surman also looked in the running for a starting place.

While we pondered what Eddie Howe might do, the club was about to surprise us with a new loan signing in the shape of Harry Wilson from Liverpool. I was thrilled 'Bournemouth has added some excitement to the season ahead with the loan signing of Harry Wilson. He's another young Welsh international who will be a great addition, while the Cherries wait for David Brooks to recover his fitness. The scoring power of the Cherries suddenly looks a lot stronger, as long as they are going to keep their other forward players, but the deal could signal that Jordon Ibe is free to join Leicester, or that Bournemouth has decided that Ryan Fraser could yet leave the club in this window.

My fears about Jordon Ibe and Ryan Fraser came to nothing, but the signing of Harry Wilson was a superb cover for the injured David Brooks. I wasn't just enthusiastic about the signing, I was starting to wonder what Harry might be able to deliver. 'Signing the hot property of Harry Wilson, 22, after the strong season he had in the Championship last year with Derby should have Bournemouth fans salivating. The signing is yet another deal cut with Liverpool who seem to be the go-to club for Bournemouth. The exciting aspect for me is the quality of the player. Bournemouth has left it late to bring in a player that will get fans jumping off their seat. Wilson is the kind of player that many other clubs would have loved to have attracted, and it is a credit to the Bournemouth recruitment staff that they managed to get the player.'

But, as usual, I was looking ahead and wondered

what the signing of Harry Wilson would mean for the shape of the team. 'There should be quite a few appearances of Ryan Giggs (Welsh manager) at Dean Court with Harry Wilson and Chris Mepham looking to get games, and while it is only a loan, Bournemouth could well have signed the player that the pundits are going to be talking about all the time when the Cherries play. It does mean a real possible shake-up in Bournemouth's starting line-up. Who will be axed to enable Bournemouth to have two Wilson's on the pitch?'

The midfield was just one area of competition. Equally as baffling was what Eddie Howe would do about the goalkeeping position. I thought Artur Boruc was in pole position, but Eddie had played his cards close to his chest and was about to surprise us all.

By the 10 August, matters had turned to which of the new players were most likely to make a start against Sheffield United in the first match of the new season. The permutations of what Eddie Howe could do for the line-up kept spinning around in my head.

'I fear we may have been robbed of wholesale changes for a couple of reasons. Lloyd Kelly may well have got the nod against Sheffield United if he hadn't become injured. Daniels is now being fast-tracked and will probably pip Diego Rico to the left-back position, as long as Adam Smith is kept on the right. Meanwhile, Adam Smith is the problem for Jack Stacey. Are we saying the Ex-Luton man is better than

Adam Smith already? I want to see a right-back defend well as well as get forward, and it may take Stacey a little while to get the balance right in the Premier League, whereas Adam Smith has plenty of experience now at the top level.

The central midfield position that Philip Billing will be after is going to be a close call. Does Eddie Howe trust the new player to be a step up on Andrew Surman, or does he play it safe and give time for Billing to bed in? This one Howe might have to sleep on, and it could go either way I think, although it wouldn't be a surprise if Surman is given the first match. Experienced heads are a good thing to have on the first day when some matches can get a bit overheated. Kris Temple, of *BBC Radio Solent*, also pointed out that Billing might not be as fit as he'd like, having not done as much training as some of the other players while at Huddersfield. Billing could always be used as a sub to push the game in the second half.

# Chapter 2. August 2019 – The new boys & the Champions

The 10 August soon came around and the preparations were over. This was a big day for AFC Bournemouth and Sheffield United, as both wanted to get off to a great start in the toughest league in the world. My eyes went straight to Bournemouth's line-up to see who had made the starting 11.

 'There were a few surprises in the Bournemouth team with Aaron Ramsdale making his Premier League debut and Philip Billing starting in central midfield, while Diego Rico won the spot for the left-back position,' I wrote on *Cherry Chimes*. 'Just as noteworthy were the absentees - new signings Arnaut Danjuma and Jack Stacey didn't make the 18-man squad, and Harry Wilson ended up spectating on the subs bench.'

The match didn't go quite as we had hoped. It was a reminder that no game is easy in this league. The introduction to my match report told the story in a few simple lines. 'Bournemouth entertained Sheffield United at a blustery Dean Court. The puff went out of the Cherries though by the end of the game. They had held a 1-0 lead from the 62nd minute when Chris Mepham broke the deadlock by stabbing home the ball, after a free kick knockdown, that saw Callum Wilson's shot rebound to him. But it had been Aaron Ramsdale who had been the busier of the keepers for much of the game. While he looked a great bet to get his first clean sheet in the Premier League, Billy Sharp stole in at the back post to give the league newcomers a well-earned point. Bournemouth were left to reflect that they hadn't found it easy to get forward and to break away from their sideways passing game.

The match had got away from AFC Bournemouth and there was no hiding from that. 'Bournemouth will consider this as two points dropped at home, having been just two minutes, plus extra-time away from the three points. But on balance, the point was a fair result. Sheffield United had matters well organised and nullified Bournemouth's attack. Ramsdale had to make several saves to keep United from going ahead early on. Sheffield created many chances while Bournemouth only created one good chance from which they scored. Why Howe didn't change the formation or change the creative side of the team is something he may have thought about post-match. The game was finally balanced when the Cherries were 1-0 up, and Howe clearly felt that the side could hold out. The problem was a moment of poor concentration and Sheffield United took their

# THE NEWBOYS & THE CHAMPIONS    35

deserved point.

'We can say Bournemouth missed the inspiration of David Brooks, but Howe could have put Harry Wilson on to try and take the game further away from Sheffield United. Settling for holding out for a 1-0 win is always risky, and this one didn't pay off,' I added.

Aaron Ramsdale had been the big plus point and I made sure that readers of *Cherry Chimes* knew that. 'I was pleased to see that Aaron Ramsdale won the goalkeeping competition to start the new season. He wasn't the man who I expected to be picked, and yet I welcomed Eddie Howe's confidence in him and the message it will have given the whole squad that places can be taken from the established players if you are good enough.'

I think I had discovered a new hero for AFC Bournemouth and in subsequent matches, I'd be raving even more about Aaron. 'Ramsdale made some excellent saves from David McGoldrick and Callum Robinson in the first half and by having the early saves it helped him grow in confidence. I like the stature Ramsdale portrays in goal. He doesn't take his eyes off play and is always alert to breaks from the opposition, while his anticipation is superb. The big kicks and passing from the back are also something that I expect gave him the edge over the other keepers, but his big test now is to hold on to the shirt.'

Digesting the 1-1 draw with Sheffield United had me searching for where Eddie needed to improve the team for next time out. Creativity was something I felt was needed, and a player that could perhaps supply that was new signing Harry Wilson. 'Harry Wilson is going to be keen to play and Howe obviously sees him playing in the team, and it was perhaps the creative spark that Bournemouth lacked against Sheffield United that started to get the home crowd annoyed about the performance.

'Whether Howe rethinks his attacking options with Jordon Ibe or Harry Wilson, he has to find something that gives Bournemouth more of a spark in and around the box for the next match,' I added.

The first away game against newly-promoted Aston Villa would be a more favourable result for the Cherries. Bournemouth still had to fight hard for their 1-2 win on 17 August in front of a crowd on 40,996. My match report gave a synopsis of the first win of the new campaign.

'The Cherries were given a dream start in this game with Tom Heaton leaving his foot out on Callum Wilson in the first minute, and Josh King made no mistake from the spot. New signing Harry Wilson then put Bournemouth firmly in control with a long-range pearler from 30 yards, that deflected in off Tyrone Mings and the post. Philip Billing was meanwhile losing his head with some rash challenges and Eddie Howe had to take him off at half-time.

Aston Villa fought back in the second half and a stunning goal from Douglas made for a grandstand finish. Bournemouth needed the safe hands of Ramsdale to keep Villa from snatching a point, and the Cherries did enough to hold on for their first three points of the season.

'Bournemouth made two changes to the starting line-up with Charlie Daniels replacing Diego Rico, and Harry Wilson coming on for Chris Mepham, as the Cherries switched back to a 4-4-1-1 formation. Jack Stacey also made it onto the sub's bench for the first time in a Premier League match.'

I added that 'Bournemouth had learned from last week how to cling on to a win. The fast start and quickly hit second goal gave the Cherries the platform they needed. Aston Villa had more of the possession and had been unlucky not to get something from the game. The Cherries were strong and kept Villa to long-range efforts for much of the game with Ramsdale playing out of his skin. So, it was a great first away win for AFCB at the first attempt.'

The primary thought I had after the Aston Villa match was that Philip Billing had to calm down in an AFC Bournemouth shirt.' We have a rival contender for Jefferson Lerma's yellow card haul from last season. Philip Billing may seem a pleasant giant, but we saw another side to him against Aston Villa. The central midfielder went for Aston Villa with little regard for what he left behind in the challenges, and with another referee, he could well have seen red.

'It was just as well that Eddie Howe took Billing off at half-time. It will be a hard lesson for the young Danish international to learn. He'll soon pick up that he can't afford to be overhyped, because of a few tackles that have been flying about. Once things get under your skin, it is easy to get carried away and intent on taking retribution, but AFCB can't afford that on the football pitch,' I commented.

Another aspect of the game against Aston Villa was that Bournemouth stuck away the penalty they received in that first minute. Josh King must have nerves of steel, as it was a highly pressured moment, and to get off to a great start was vital to ensure Bournemouth got something from the game.

'When your team turns up at a newly-promoted team, in front of a big crowd, and the first home game of the season for the opposition, it's going to be a nervous affair. But Bournemouth didn't accept that they should go into their shell and weather the storm. They decided to attack and take the game to Aston Villa and they duly got their rewards in the first minute,' I wrote on my blog post of 20 August.

'That platform completely turned around the afternoon for AFCB from being a problem game to a match that they had the advantage in the that they knew that if they defended well, they'd get something from the game. When everything starts to go your way, there is a love of football that injects itself into the players' play. They believe that things are going to continue going their way and they try to do the unexpected, like Harry Wilson's long-range effort that doubled the lead on 12 minutes. The adrenalin was pumping in all AFCB's players and the fans at that moment.'

One player that was just super excited to be back out on the field was Charlie Daniels. This was his comeback match, having been injured since the previous season. He needed to play as many minutes as he could with Lloyd Kelly side-lined in pre-season. Eddie Howe has his personal favourites, as they have been trusted over many seasons, and Daniels is one of those players. 'While Diego Rico played in the first match against Sheffield United, he couldn't hold back a fully-fit Charlie Daniels. The team is of course familiar with Daniels being at left-back. It gives the team more of a regular feel with Daniels and Fraser able to play their usual patterns of play,' I wrote on my blog post entitled 'Daniels recovers quickly for Villa start'.

Another player that was enjoying being in the starting line-up for the first time was Harry Wilson. I was very pleased that Bournemouth finally had a player who was prepared to shoot when he had a sight of goal. My praise was high indeed. 'Harry Wilson delivered against Villa with the kind of goal that made him look every bit as good as David Brooks.'

If Harry Wilson's goal at Villa Park was a sign of what was to come, he was going to have a great season. 'Although Wilson played on the right-wing, he wasn't slow to run into the central position, when space arose and, unlike many of Bournemouth's players, he was willing to take a risk – to strike the ball from distance. It is that kind of confidence and ambition that AFCB will need to break some defences. The ball flew in and Tom Heaton couldn't get near it,' I beamed.

With two games gone Bournemouth didn't have the perfect start, but the away win was something to savour. The important thing was that AFCB did get some points from the considered lesser teams that have just been promoted. Not to get anything or just a couple of draws would have been a real disappointment. Aston Villa and Sheffield United are not teams that will frighten many in the Premier League I thought at that time. But the points still had to be won, and some teams wouldn't do as well against these two teams. Little did I know that Sheffield United would have such a great season.

The importance of having some points on the board was made clear by the next visitors to Dean Court. In the build-up to the game, I was pondering over whether Eddie Howe would revert to five at the back, as he had in the previous season, when Bournemouth's failure to register a shot on goal was roundly condemned by pundits, as was the 17 per cent possession.

Trying to work out how to stop Man City was the main focus of 24 August. I felt that it was in midfield where Man City tend to establish their superiority from in game. They also just happen to have world-class finishers in Raheem Sterling, Sergio Agüero and Gabriel Jesus.

I looked at whether Eddie Howe had it in him to out-smart Pep Guardiola. I was confident that it was something that Eddie Howe was keen to prove that it could be done. 'The omens might not seem great, but I don't doubt that the personal challenge that Eddie Howe has to take points off of every manager in the Premier League is one that sits uneasily with him. It's only right that Pep Guardiola is the one manager that he is left with from the top six that has got the better of him, and it is building to a day when Howe does come out on top. There is every chance that record could be about to fall, as Howe has more and more experience and his squad is being bolstered all the time.

We also knew Man City would still be smarting from their draw with Tottenham in their previous match, when Gabriel Jesus had looked to have won the game but for a VAR decision in added time that kept the score at 2-2.

Taking on Man City would be a different affair from last season, when Eddie Howe set-up

Bournemouth to simply try and repel the attacks. Howe knew the team had to show more ambition, and that would come with taking some risks.

The only change Eddie made was to move Harry Wilson to the bench and bring in Chris Mepham to the starting line-up. But stopping Man City would take more than replacing an attacker with a defender.

'Bournemouth did all they could to get their first-ever point against Man City in the Premier League, but they had no answer to Sergio Agüero's sharp finishing and Sterling's dance through the defence,' I said on *Cherry Chimes*. 'In a frantic first half, the challenges came in thick and fast with Kyle Walker and Ederson grateful to only see yellow cards. Bournemouth fell behind to an incisive run up the left side and Agüero tucked away his shot just inside the post in the six-yard box.

'The game looked over when Raheem Sterling doubled the lead by stabbing home past Aaron Ramsdale, but a terrific free kick from Harry Wilson pegged City back to 1-2 before the break. While the Bournemouth fans did what they could to lift the home team, it was Agüero who wrapped up the win with the final goal to leave Bournemouth fans dreaming of what could have been.

So, it was another defeat, but would it be damaging? I wasn't so disappointed with the way the Cherries had played the game. The talk after the game was not that Bournemouth had been swept away, but more than Harry Wilson had scored a stunning goal from a free kick.

The moment that led up to the free kick gave no warning of what was about to happen. It had looked like Bournemouth would be 0-2 down at half-time. Here is a bit of the live commentary I put on the blog. 'Six minutes of added time go up. Wilson is fouled on the edge of the box by Aymeric Laporte as he tried to turn. Harry Wilson has slammed the ball into the top right corner, off the post, from the free kick! Amazing shot 1-2. Bournemouth are back in this.'

It was a moment of false hope, but at least Bournemouth had shown some resistance. Bournemouth had put up a fight, but Man City remained far too strong. It was just a few moments when City managed to unlock the door that will haunt Eddie Howe, but he'll know his team put up a strong performance against the Champions. The analysis of the game soon showed where the Cherries needed to improve. The shot count for Bournemouth was very encouraging with 10 shots and seven on target. Not converting more of those seven shots on target proved costly. Limiting Man City to 19 shots meant about 10 each half, but City only had five shots on target. The problem is that City took three of those five chances.

Harry Wilson was voted player of the month for August. He had announced his arrival on the south coast with a couple of stunning goals and he was enjoying the limelight. I was convinced that Wilson was another player that Bournemouth had done well to capture.

'We have only seen Harry Wilson in a couple of games for AFC Bournemouth, but we can already see that he is something special. I said on *Cherry Chimes*. 'It is not every player that can come into a new team and have the confidence to take a free kick from the regulars, and then go and slot it in the top corner. Harry Wilson wants to make a name for himself while he is at AFCB, and he has set about doing that in some style.'

'It was a surprise to me that Eddie did not pick Harry to start against Man City, but he's going to have some pressure on him now to pick him for the match against Leicester City,' I added.

Before then, the Cherries would be looking at another cup run in the Carabao Cup. The team was going to have changes and the left-back position was of mounting interest, as Charlie Daniels had suffered a season-ending injury on his knee against Man City. It would be down to Diego Rico to step up and show that he was the player who Howe could rely on. It was a big opportunity for Rico, but he had been more than patient and would rapidly become a fans favourite, despite having had such a quiet start to his Bournemouth career.

Before the next league game, Bournemouth would have the chance to see how some of the other squad members were doing, as the Carabao Cup matches began.

Forest Green Rovers were riding high in third in League Two, when they faced the Cherries at Dean Court, in the second round of the Carabao Cup on 28 August. Bournemouth fielded what I suppose fans would call the second 11 with Mark Travers, Jack Stacey, Chris Mepham, Jack Simpson, Diego Rico, Gavin Kilkenny, Andrew Surman and Jordon Ibe joining the more regular first-team faces of Harry Wilson, Dominic Solanke and Callum Wilson. It wasn't long before Bournemouth had added three more big names to the players on the field, as Forest Green Rovers battled their way to a 0-0 draw in 90 minutes. While Fraser, King and Billing had reinforced the Cherries in the second half, they were unable to beat Forest Green Rover's keeper Joe Wollacott.

In the end, it would be all about the keepers, as the penalty competition would sort out the team to go through. Mark Travers came out triumphant having made three penalty saves to see Bournemouth through 3-0 on spot-kicks.

Any joy would be short-lived. The league programme span round quickly with the last game before the international break against Leicester City, away on 31 August. It was a difficult day for the Cherries with plenty of defensive frailties to worry about. The early setback was particularly hard to swallow. Jamie Vardy lobbed Leicester ahead in the

11th minute after a bit of a mix-up between Chris Mepham, Steve Cook and Aaron Ramsdale who all made it easier for Vardy.

Callum Wilson got off the mark just three minutes later. He made an incisive run and finished off the post, before Youri Tielemans tapped in another goal off the far post just before half-time. Then Leicester extended their lead when Vardy latched on to the ball from Tielemans in the box to make it 3-1 after Bournemouth had several chances to clear. Chris Mepham had inadvertently scuffed his clearance before the third goal, and the ping-pong attempted clearances only led to a heavier scoreline.

What narked a lot of Bournemouth fans was that Tielemans had got away with a bad foul on the back of Callum Wilson's ankle at the start of the second half, and might have counted himself lucky to still be on the pitch. The defeat certainly hurt, 'The longer the game went on the worse it got, with Leicester far more positive in the final third. Bournemouth needed to defend much better and Howe can't expect his team to have to score four to get something away from home.'

Having a couple of weeks to mull over the performance was perhaps not what the fans needed, but Bournemouth did need it to re-organise. The Cherries had come up against a good side and had been torn apart – it simply hadn't been a close contest. Slipping to 15th in the league wasn't the worst of it, as Adam Smith had pulled up in the second half with a hamstring strain and would be out for a few weeks.

I had to reflect on the game and it didn't paint a happy picture. 'Bournemouth are too often ready to drop their heads when things aren't going their way I feel. I am sure the players are trying, but there needs to be more fight about the team when they go behind. In previous seasons we have seen great fightbacks and real steel about this team, but I am worried whether it is there this season.

'Howe likes to attack, which I commend him for, but if the team is going to concede three or more goals every week, how can he expect his strikers to win many games for the team? The first thing that every manager has to get right is the defence. You make yourself hard to beat and build from there. I feel the foundations are not in place at the moment at the back, and unless the team works at this part of its game more religiously, there will be more days like we saw at Leicester City.'

# Chapter 3. September – The Carabao Cup goes for a Burton

The international break allowed AFC Bournemouth to do some business. Asmir Begović was to be loaned out to Azerbaijan team Qarabağ Ağdam FK, until January 2020. I was pleased that a decision had been made on Begović, and that he could try to regain his form elsewhere. 'It was no doubt important that Howe found a club for Asmir, as it didn't look like he would be involved this season at AFCB. He didn't need to be training when AFCB have a good selection of other keepers. Asmir's fall from grace has been fairly quick, but in the Premier League, it is important to play with the best keeper you can get. The young keepers of Aaron Ramsdale and Mark Travers now look set to be the standard for AFCB keepers in the next few years.'

The team was also leaking goals and a remedy was needed. But how would Eddie Howe find a remedy with most of his first-choice players at the back, needing time in the treatment centre?

'The holes in the team are starting to show. Eddie Howe keeps shuffling the pack, but as soon as he does, another player picks up an injury. Yet, we are only just a month into the new season, and teams that get a lot of injuries usually struggle to pick up points. We are starting to see that scenario at Bournemouth. It does seem unfair that wherever Howe looks to strengthen his team, he finds that injuries pop up in places where he least needs them. Last season it was in central midfield and now it is in defence, where it is worse when players drop out of the team, as the whole solidity of the side comes under pressure.

'If Bournemouth were a blanket, it would be looking more like a patchwork quilt at the moment, but the problem is that quilt doesn't cover the pitch very well.'

I was wondering where Eddie Howe would find the positivity to take the team forward. 'The need to see Lewis Cook and perhaps Junior Stanislas putting on their shirts again is something that Bournemouth fans might not have felt was that pressing at the start of August, but the team needs a bit of quality and new energy and these two players just might provide some of that.'

We all knew what Howe needed but would the players return quickly? 'If Howe can get a couple of players back though by the end of the international break, and I include Simon Francis in that, then the mood in the camp might well pick up as might the results,' I commented.

Fans wanted to see what Eddie Howe would do at the back with Charlie Daniels and Adam Smith out injured. Would he give Diego Rico and Jack Stacey a run in the team?

Two days before the match with Everton, I remarked on Mark Lawrenson's pundit prediction that Bournemouth would win. 'Mark Lawrenson doesn't often like to give AFCB a winning prediction, but I see he can't help kick the Everton fans in the teeth as a former Liverpool player – you have to laugh! Despite Bournemouth's soft-centre, he has gone for a Cherries 2-1 victory over the Toffees on Sunday. While Lawro likes to hammer AFCB for their defensive frailties, he might just be right that there will be a few goals in this game. I'll take his prediction anyway because he won't expect AFCB to win many times this season.'

We hadn't seen a clean sheet yet and I was more concerned that Aaron Ramsdale might be starting to feel he was not being lucky in goal. A clean sheet would do wonders for Ramsdale and the back four, but Bournemouth hadn't been playing well enough at this stage and Ramsdale was under no illusion that his position could soon come under pressure.

I detailed the mood ahead of the next match with Everton. 'In a week that we have seen Mark Travers win his first senior cap for the Republic of Ireland squad, the focus on AFCB's keepers is as high as ever. The competition for the top spot hasn't slowed, despite the departure of Asmir Begović.

It was a fresh-looking AFCB starting 11 at the Everton match. Fraser and Lerma were rested on the bench to give Dominic Solanke and Lewis Cook a start for the first time this season. Diego Rico and Jack Stacey also came into the team for Chris Mepham and the injured Adam Smith.

Bournemouth got the important first goal from a set-piece when a cross came off Josh King at the far post and Callum Wilson could simply head in from close range. But the lead only lasted 19 minutes, as Richarlison crossed for the visitors a minute before half-time and Dominic Calvert-Lewin rose above Steve Cook to head in for 1-1.

The game swung very much in Bournemouth's favour when Harry Wilson was subbed and Ryan Fraser came on. The Scotsman's free kick, a few minutes after coming on, was deflected in off Fabian Delph, but Fraser was allowed to keep the goal. Matters were then finalised when Diego Rico chipped a ball over Everton's defence, on the left side, and Callum Wilson broke free to lob Jordan Pickford and make it 3-1 to the Cherries.

'Bournemouth found their swagger in the second half and were helped with some poor defending by Everton. Callum Wilson has shot to the top of Bournemouth's goal scorers and looked hungry for more. It was Lewis Cook and Josh King that impressed me most though of the outfield players, while Ramsdale was again steady in goal. This was an encouraging performance.'

Eddie Howe was adamant that the first win at home against Everton was a defining moment in the Cherries season. I was equally enthused by what the Cherries had just done. 'Bournemouth would have been hovering just above the bottom three if they hadn't beaten Everton. By changing the team to get the result, Eddie now has a happy bunch of players all eager to try and get into the game for the Friday night fixture against Southampton.'

I added that 'the match against Everton was not all perfect by any means. Before Bournemouth took the lead, Everton had hit the bar and looked the most likely to score, but a corner kick gave Callum Wilson his chance to add to his goals this season. Heading in the goal showed how he doesn't care how the goals come, as long as they come to him.'

Even more evident was that Lewis Cook's return had been massive for the team. He dominated the early part of the match and he looked like he had never been away.'

'Unbeknown to us he [Lewis Cook] had two games in the weeks running up to his first league match and was able to play a good hour against Everton. Eddie Howe said his team needed him to play and his impact could be seen right from the start.

'The crowd enjoyed seeing Lewis back in action and the way they responded to his every touch will have given him an even better feeling inside, which certainly helped his game. For me, he was the man of the match, because he shouldn't have been that good coming back into the team after having a horrendous injury. But he was brave and was pleased to start, which was throwing him in at the deep end.'

While everything was suddenly looking better in the centre- of midfield, there was reason to believe that Harry Wilson had lost a bit of form. I also wasn't sure that playing Dominic Solanke next to Callum Wilson was the surest way of getting more goals, with Josh King out on the wing.

I put Harry Wilson's difficulties just down to the number of games he was playing. 'In the last two matches against Leicester City and Everton, the form of Harry Wilson has dipped a fair bit from the opening two games of the season. He also had a tough time playing for Wales, which begs the question of whether he needs to be pulled out of the fire for a game or two, just to reset his mental attitude and get him back on the right path. He has looked a little lost in the last two games, but perhaps that is only to be expected after the two sensational opening games he had.'

Solanke's failure to score would be a constant

issue I expected unless he felt truly confident about being picked for the starting 11. 'It was a great day for Callum against Everton, but Dominic is still waiting to break his Bournemouth goal duck in the Premier League. So, will Solanke be a permanent fixture in the starting line-up? 'Eddie Howe chose Solanke to play against Everton, because of his last 20-minute performance at Leicester City. I hope Eddie Howe will give Solanke a bit more of a chance than just this one game to see if he can make the grade. He did not have many opportunities in the Everton match, and the well-hit strike he had in the first half was well saved by Jordan Pickford.'

One player who had done well against Everton was Jack Stacey and I was pleased to remind people of that. 'Jack Stacey finally made his Premier League debut and he played very well against Alex Iwobi, who he marked for most of the afternoon. I am sure Eddie worked all week and more with Jack to make sure he was ready for Everton, and it was a bold move playing Jack with Harry Wilson ahead of him, as the two won't have played that much football together.

No matter how many games players had played for Bournemouth, I didn't doubt that Eddie Howe would get them up for the next game on a Friday night because it was that lot down the road – Southampton. The game was not only intriguing because the game was our derby, but the winner would jump right up the table, such was the tightness of the league.

'They [Southampton] have picked up the same amount of points as the Cherries from their first six games, and the winner of this match will feel that it will be three very significant points towards what half of the table they finish in.'

Whoever won the match would go third at least overnight, with the majority of the fixtures to follow over the weekend. Bournemouth hadn't won away at Southampton since 1953, so fans travelled more in hope than expectation. Now the 20 September 2019 would be a date to remember when another record was broken by Eddie Howe's men.

Eddie Howe only made one change to the winning team against Everton. Lewis Cook was managed by moving him to the bench, after his impressive comeback from injury in the last match, and Jefferson Lerma took his place in central midfield. Ryan Fraser found himself still stuck on the bench, nursing a bit of a knock, while Josh King kept his place on the wing so that Solanke could try and break his scoring duck upfront. Harry Wilson also kept his place, despite recently falling short of his great performances in earlier games. Bournemouth wore their all-new, dark, navy-blue, strip for the first time this season.

The game went better than expected for Bournemouth fans from the off, with Nathan Aké heading in from a corner in the 10th minute to give the Cherries the lead. That lead was then doubled on 35 minutes when Harry Wilson swept the ball past Angus Gunn from a pass from Philip Billing. It could have been a bigger lead at half-time, but Josh King had a goal ruled out by VAR for being marginally offside. The second half looked like being a tighter affair when Steve Cook made a poorly timed challenge on Ché Adams and a penalty was awarded to the Saints, from which James Ward-Prowse scored. Bournemouth fans would have the last laugh though. Angus Gunn and Jan Bednarek ran into each other and left Callum Wilson with the goal at his mercy to make it 1-3 in the fifth minute of added time.

Philip Billing was my man of the match, but I could easily have picked Aaron Ramsdale or Josh King. This was a superb Bournemouth performance and we looked ahead with optimism. 'There was one team that was willing to leave everything on the pitch to get a win at St Marys. AFCB may have found it tough going in the second half, but their resolve was outstanding,' I commented.

'Now the hoodoo has finally fallen and Bournemouth's players can hold their heads up high. They were magnificent and the running power of King and Billing were fundamental reasons why they won the game. Add in the sharp saves of Aaron Ramsdale and the defending of Nathan Aké and Jack Stacey, and for once Bournemouth looked like a team that was organised and galvanised in their single task.'

Like most Bournemouth fans, I took particular delight in the Cherries' third goal of the night at Southampton. It was a calamity for the Saints. 'Southampton were going to lose the game and it probably just put a bit more gloss on the scoreline for Bournemouth. But it's the kind of goal that will get rolled out for years to come now, as the goal that made Southampton look extremely silly in the south coast derby and that gifted Callum Wilson a goal,' I reported.

Before we could gloat too much though, we would see our side go crashing out of the Carabao Cup to League One opposition Burton Albion. The match on 25 September was a third round tie. A tie that Bournemouth thought they would comfortably progress from. However, Burton had been in good form, even if their match lighting would not be as sturdy. Oliver Sarkic volleyed the home side ahead on 15 minutes, while the failing light system put the continuation of the game in doubt. The match resumed after a half-hour delay. It turned out to be Burton's night when Nathan Broadhead made it 2-0 from a cross on 72 minutes to send Bournemouth crashing out of the cup.

After the game, I talked about how rotation was not always a good thing for the team. While Eddie Howe wanted to rest some key players, it was more than just a game for the Brewers. 'The problem was that AFCB are now big fish and the Brewers would see this game as their cup final, even if it was only in front of 2500 fans,' I stated.

'The fact that the lights went out is quite fitting. Bournemouth's game faded out if you like before it had started, with Burton Albion scoring as early as the 15th minute. AFCB can make excuses about the lights failing and it disrupting their rhythm, but on the evidence of the first half, Burton had been well worth their lead at half-time and Travers was the busier of the two keepers by some distance.'

What was needed was another game to put the embarrassment behind the players. It was no good moaning about a missed opportunity. Eddie Howe could give reasons for the defeat, but it didn't make it look any better. 'Eddie was keen to stress that he played a young team in the cup and that those players need to get a game at some point. Eddie will likely have learned a lot about his players from the last match, and he'll want to get back to winning ways,' I summarised.

It was West Ham United who would visit Dean Court next, but before they played I answered some questions on AFC Bournemouth for the *West Ham Till I Die* blog.

WTID: For a short while, last weekend, Bournemouth were sitting third in the table, after two great wins against Everton and your south coast rivals Southampton, you must be thinking that you've got this Premier League cracked?

CC: Hardly! Bournemouth has been notorious for finding difficulty where there was none, and just because we have had a run of a couple of wins, it doesn't guarantee you anything in this league. I am optimistic about the home form holding up, but as usual AFC Bournemouth has not kept a clean sheet in the league. It puts a lot of pressure on the team knowing they have to score at least two goals to win a match.

WTID: Last season West Ham ended up 10th and Bournemouth 14th: this weekend we play each other sitting 5th and 6th respectively, where do you think Bournemouth and West Ham will both finish the season?

CC: I was pretty conservative in my expectation for Bournemouth this season knowing in the summer that there were a lot of players still looking to get back from injury and that they wouldn't even be in contention until October/November. So, I predicted a 12th place finish for Bournemouth. I didn't think about West Ham that much, but I don't see why they can't improve on last season and finish about eighth.

WTID: Talking of last season, what were the highlights for you?

CC: Honestly, it had to be the 4-0 home win against Chelsea. We were completely outplayed first half but got in 0-0. Then, the counter-attacking football that was played in the second half was unbelievable, just about everything came off and we had a comfortable win over a top six-club.

WTID: Conversely what were the moments of deep despair?

CC: I suppose losing to Fulham 0-1 at home gave me pretty much an equal feeling of despair. But you couldn't get much worse than a former player coming back to score against you in added time for Newcastle to earn a 2-2 draw against us – thanks, Matt Ritchie!

WTID: How do you judge Eddie Howe's signings of the summer? Do you think you are a better team? Although we are barely into the season, who looks like becoming a Bournemouth regular?

CC: The jury is still out on some of the summer signings. Jack Stacey seems to be doing okay at right-back, but it is a big jump up for him from League One. Lloyd Kelly, we have only seen in friendlies and we need him back fit to give us some left-back options. Arnaut Danjuma is a left-sided winger who again we saw in pre-season and then he got injured so he should be back soon. The star performers are Philip

Billing in centre-midfield, who has been improving every game, and Harry Wilson, who has come in on loan from Liverpool. Harry has a fierce shot on him. Whereas many of our players are slow to look up and shoot around the box, it always seems the first thing on Harry Wilson's mind and he's very accurate.

I'd say we are stronger in that we have a solid crop of midfield players, but we are lacking top quality striker replacements on the bench, and I don't see that the defence is much stronger than last season, because Adam Smith and Steve Cook and Nathan Aké are still starters if they are fit.

WTID: There is a lot of chat about Callum Wilson being a target for a bigger team, how do Bournemouth fans rate him, and how do you compare him to Josh King?

CC: Callum does a lot of work in making runs and playing others in, as well as getting on the end of moves. He has become a better finisher in the box and Bournemouth now relies on him to get the majority of goals. Josh King is playing on the wing at the moment and he is a bundle of energy when he puts his mind to it. When he has an off-game though, you'll struggle to find him on the pitch.

WTID: Already the Premier League looks like being a two-horse race between Liverpool and Manchester

City: can you see this changing? Which two other teams will join them to make up the top four come May? (Prediction in order)

CC: Agreed, Liverpool and Man City are going to fight it out amongst themselves. I hope Liverpool do it this time. I did expect Leicester to be up there, but I had thought Wolves would be doing much better, even with the burden of the Europa League. Still, it leaves room for teams like West Ham and Bournemouth to try and crash the party, but I don't think Everton will be contenders for Europe this season. If I have to pick a top four, I'll say Chelsea third and Spurs fourth.

WTID: Who are your favourites for the drop at this early stage of the season?

CC: I had said at the start of the season Brighton, Sheffield United and Aston Villa. I don't see much reason to change my mind yet.
WTID: Which West Ham players, if any would you like to see turning out for Bournemouth, and why?

CC: Andriy Yarmolenko has had a good impact for you already, so I'm looking to see how good he is on the ball. But I suppose most of us will be very watchful of the big singing Sébastien Haller, who has made it difficult for defences.

WTID: Which two players of any clubs in the country do you most admire? Reasons?

CC: That's a tough one. I won't include AFC Bournemouth players. I'd probably say Ashley Barnes at Burnley as he is an unfashionable striker, who just has a habit of sticking the ball away with no fuss, and I'll go for defender Patrick Van Arnaut at Crystal Palace, who has great pace and a good left foot shot on him. There you go, I kept clear of Liverpool and Man City too!

WTID: How will Bournemouth line up against West Ham on Saturday? Team & Formation?

CC: I expect an unchanged side, even if Lewis Cook is going to be pushing for a start.

Ramsdale
Stacey, S Cook, Aké, Rico
H Wilson, Lerma, Billing, King
C Wilson, Solanke

WTID: You've had two wins on the bounce, are you confident that you can make it three out of three against West Ham? Prediction for score?

CC: I'll go for a 2-1 home win. We always concede at least one goal, but the team is going well with six goals in the last two games.

With my chat with *West Ham Till I Die* over, it was down to the verdict and the match result. West Ham was a team in form and would be in third place after the game, while Bournemouth would drop back to seventh. It could have been so much more than a point, but the 2-2 draw was at least something to take into the next game. Bournemouth almost had West Ham and the result in the bag, but a missed opportunity from Callum Wilson and a VAR offside decision prevented them from getting a 3-1 lead. Worse still, West Ham came back to grab a point that was probably just about deserved.

'The Cherries had come from behind when Yarmolenko had put West Ham ahead on 10 minutes with a sharp shot into the corner. Josh King had got the Cherries back on level terms with a scrambled goal after a corner that needed a VAR decision before it was finally given. The game looked to have swung Bournemouth's way when Callum Wilson swivelled to find the bottom corner of the net just a minute into the second half. But West Ham put the pressure on Bournemouth's defence, which eventually gave way when Aaron Cresswell rescued a point late on,' I reported.

I was disappointed but not unrealistic about the

result. It was a better performance than we had seen mid-week against Burton Albion. 'A draw was not a bad result, when Yarmolenko and Pablo Fornals had a lot of the game for the Hammers. But a VAR disallowed goal, Callum Wilson's one-on-one and Creswell's tug on Josh King in the box could have given Bournemouth the edge if one of those instances had turned out differently. Still, Ramsdale again showed why he is Bournemouth's number one and Jack Stacey had his best game for the Cherries, I said.

The main talking point after the West Ham game was the implementation of VAR. West Ham had been hopeful of Josh King's goal being overturned. Bournemouth fans waited for an age for the decision. It spoils the moment and it was the first time that the home fans had experienced that kind of delay for a decision.

I have not been a fan of VAR in the Premier League, but it was excellently employed in the 2018 World Cup in Russia. There are probably reasons for that, but I felt the whole discussion was showing the Premier League in a bad light.

'It's funny how the fans call for consistency with refereeing and that is what many thought we would get with VAR. It's not VAR that is the problem though.' I stressed. 'It is doing what it was set up for, making calls black and white. It's the implementation of it and the interpretation of those rules - the human factor – which is causing most of the problems.

'Through gritted teeth, we have to see things through with VAR. I've kept away from it for as long as I can this season, but I'm not confident that AFCB won't have further reasons to be annoyed with VAR this season.'

# Chapter 4. October – The goalless month

The start of the season might not have gone as well as the previous one, but the Cherries were sitting in seventh place after 11 games and were equal on points with Chelsea and Arsenal. Bournemouth had been scoring freely enough, with 13 goals from those early games, but things were about to change.

Bournemouth has always been seen as an attacking side and has won many converts, because of the way they go at teams with no fear. Eddie Howe had indulged in the summer with his love of wingers and brought in Harry Wilson on loan. While it may have seemed that Eddie was doubling up on surnames for his players with Cooks and Wilsons, he had allowed Brad Smith to go out to play in America for a couple of seasons, and Brad Smith would later go on loan to Cardiff, while Adam Smith remained a frontline AFCB player. The name selection game was whether Harry Wilson was the best pick for the right wing? He had started against West Ham, but had been subbed for Arnaud Danjuma after 77 minutes. Now I wondered if Danjuma could oust Harry Wilson from the team from the start in the next game against Arsenal.

The matter came to the fore with me on 3 October on the blog, 'I've been watching Harry Wilson as closely as I can in recent games to see how well he is fitting in. He has been scoring, but there is something that doesn't quite sit well, and I think it is that he might be better playing in the hole, behind the main striker, where he can influence play.

'I am sure that Harry Wilson has been brought in as cover for David Brooks and that is how Eddie Howe needs to use him at the moment. It's a problem of numbers with Junior Stanislas and David Brooks being unavailable. When that changes though, there will be less need to force Harry to play out on the right wing and I think it could be very exciting to see him play through the middle, with Fraser and Brooks supplying the wing play that will make Bournemouth a much more balanced attacking force.'

Another Bournemouth player was also receiving plenty of attention. Callum Wilson was being touted as the signing that the Red Devils needed and *SkySports* was indicating that Ole Gunnar Solskjaer was interested in the forward. I was sure that Callum would be loving the headlines but wasn't sure if he would be that keen to head to Manchester if the offer materialised in the January window.

'Should Man United come in with a big offer in January, Callum Wilson would have a big decision to make. Should he follow in the footsteps of Ted MacDougall and smash his salary and AFCB's transfer record? Usually, the answer would be a straight yes, but he'll have to consider if he wants to be a part of what is a Man United rebuilding job. Yes, Man United is a massive club, perhaps the biggest in the world, but in January they could be looking at struggling to make the top 10. Ole Gunnar Solskjaer could be sacked and is perhaps hoping that a signing like Wilson is his best way of staying in the job. Joining Man United is not like joining any other club. Callum would have to reconcile himself with the pressure of such a big move.'

I added that: 'Being a big fish in a little pool is perhaps what he has become at AFCB. The transfer fee would go a long way to increasing AFCB's profits for the season and they could be near to safety by the end of January. But losing Callum would be a huge blow for the club and Eddie Howe's aspirations of building the team around Wilson. While AFCB might be able to say no to a low bid, they may have to reconsider if there is a sudden bidding war for Callum's services.'

On 3 October, we were also told that Diego Rico had been named player of the month for September. I had been blown away with how well Rico had done since coming into the team to replace the luckless Charlie Daniels.

Meanwhile, big news came with the club's

announcement that Council approval had been given for construction to start at the Canford Manor Training Complex. It has been a long-time ambition of Eddie Howe and Jason Tindall to build a special training centre as a legacy for the club's time in the Premier League. Things were beginning to come to fruition now.

Bournemouth's next task would be to see if they could get their first win at the Emirates. It was a game where Bournemouth just didn't get going in the first half. They slipped behind to a corner kick header from David Luiz on nine minutes. It was frustrating as the side showed in the second half that they could more than compete. Gamesmanship got Arsenal home, but Bournemouth just didn't get enough possession in and around Arsenal's box and Leno had few saves to make. A draw might have been a fairer result but it was not to be.

Eddie Howe said it through gritted teeth I think. Bournemouth let a soft goal in during the first 10 minutes because he mentioned that they could not afford a start like that before the game. He was right, it took all of the first half to recover from that. It was a huge step back in conceding the first goal, and the Cherries didn't react well enough early on in the game.

The corner itself was driven towards the near post and if Bournemouth were zonal marking they didn't get tight enough to David Luiz, who seemed to get away from Callum Wilson and had a clear header to pass Ramsdale. The clean sheet just doesn't seem to be coming, and yet AFCB didn't look like conceding a second goal all game.

Bournemouth got closer to Arsenal in the second half and could have got something from the game, but there was no confidence in the finishing. It sometimes takes a defeat like this to get the players up for the next game, and AFCB's players will have a fortnight to reflect on a missed opportunity to get their first win at Arsenal.

'The most glaring opportunity during the Arsenal match for Bournemouth probably fell to Callum Wilson, when he beat two players, on the edge of the box, rounded Leno but ran out of an angle, looking for Josh King just three yards out,' I recalled.

If that was frustrating and deserved a goal, there was also Dominic Solanke's headed miss in the first half, when Rico put in a superb ball for him to head wide unchallenged. Callum Wilson had a half-chance right at the death as well, but could only shoot right at Leno. It was that kind of day. The ball just didn't run for Bournemouth in this game.'

The other discussion after the Arsenal defeat centred on the substitutions. 'The last period of the game against Arsenal could have gone better. Bournemouth made changes with Danjuma and Simon Francis coming on as the final throw of the dice, but it was baffling to some fans why Lewis Cook was not put on,' I wrote.

'What I don't know is if Jack Stacey felt he had run out of steam or was injured. Putting on a right-back made sense if Howe didn't feel safe going to a back three late on. Danjuma was an attacking move, but Simon Francis will have looked a negative sub to many.

'After the international break, AFCB may be in a better position in terms of team selection choices. Eddie Howe will need that as one or two are not looking quite on their game at the moment. If the goals are drying up, AFCB will need some faces on the bench who might be able to turn games like the Arsenal match around.'

The international break gave fans the chance to remember how the club had been transformed in the last seven years. It was in October 2012, when Eddie Howe and Jason Tindall had returned to Bournemouth from Burnley, in their second spell as the management team at the club. I was pleased to hear that Eddie also mentioned that he would not want fans to forget that he spent some 20 months at Burnley and that that period was so important for him to be where he is today. It is what I felt when writing *Eddie Had A Dream*. The chapter I wrote entitled 'Dressed in Claret' highlights the challenges Eddie had as a young manager in the Championship for the first time, saddled with a club that had been in the Premier League, but needed rebuilding. The period did not go so well for Eddie, but when he returned to Bournemouth, he had so much more knowledge of how a strong Championship team would need to operate. Working with players that had been in the Premier League will have given him more ideas of the qualities he needed to find in players going forward.

While we were reminiscing, there was also lots of positives about the future. Aaron Ramsdale had made a terrific start to life in the Premier League and Harry Wilson was an unusual, but lively, interviewer of the goalkeeper for *AFCBTV* on his recent performances. I couldn't let the moment pass and had a few comments on the matter.

'The affection that Aaron has built up with the AFCB fans already though is tremendous. We think he is England's No 1, and I don't think it will be long before he is thought of in that way far outside of Bournemouth.

'What I see is that the fans can identify with Ramsdale. He is a character. You have to have a screw slightly loose to play in goal, and the main thing for Aaron at the moment should be just to enjoy playing. It is a fantastic achievement for him to be playing at such a young age in the Premier League, and he looks perfectly at home there.

'Of course, Aaron has to keep his standard high and keep his professionalism when he represents the club. He can do that and be pleased with his performances when he pulls off the saves, but I see a cheeky side to him, and I expect he has to tone things down at some points. You need some loud characters in the team though. I think Aaron could be one of the players of the season. He is super confident and I hope he remains so.'

Eddie Howe was still brooding over the last defeat I was sure. I couldn't get away from his post-match comments, 'Eddie Howe promised there was more to come from the Cherries after the Arsenal game. How far short Bournemouth is of being 100 per cent is not clear, but looking back at the past eight games, can we say that AFCB played the other team off the park for 90 minutes very often?

'I'd argue the wins against Aston Villa, Southampton and Everton were all great, but were they comprehensive wins? The score lines in the Southampton and Everton games might suggest that they were, but they were fairly tight games with Everton perhaps the game where Bournemouth were most dominant. So, there is work to do.'

Addressing the ability of the team to come out of the gates fast, and be on their game from the off, was another aspect of Bournemouth's performance that was also troubling me.

'The team was flat for 45 minutes against Arsenal. They simply can't afford to do that in a home game against Norwich, who will come thinking they have every chance of getting something from this match. I am hoping Eddie does something bold to give Bournemouth a strong start and get the team pressing Norwich in their half. We can't afford another laidback game. So, if there is more to come from the Cherries, let's have it!'

A player that might also be hoping that he received more game time was Arnaut Danjuma. 'We have not seen a great deal of Arnaut Danjuma. He has come on as a late sub a couple of times, and while he is being introduced gradually, he could find that the international breaks are a great opportunity to get up to speed with what Eddie Howe wants him to do. AFCB did not say he was away on international duty, so I assume he stayed in Bournemouth.

'It is possible that Eddie may make a change or two anyway next game, with the team looking to find a way to get back to winning ways. Danjuma would be an interesting choice.'

As it happened, Eddie did make changes with Lewis Cook, Ryan Fraser and Adam Smith coming into the side, while Jack Stacey, Jefferson Lerma and Josh King were removed. King moved to the bench.

Norwich City would not be a simple game for Bournemouth. They might not have picked up any points away from home, before playing the Cherries, but they had beaten Man City at home. Still, they came into the game against Bournemouth on the back of a 1-5 home defeat to Aston Villa.

What we probably didn't expect was a 0-0 scoreline. Bournemouth hadn't had a clean sheet in their previous eight games. If anyone could be pleased it was Aaron Ramsdale in finally going 90 minutes without conceding – he certainly deserved it.

My match verdict emphasised that the Cherries just didn't do enough in the last third of the field. 'This was a game where Bournemouth would have expected to take three points, but just like the Sheffield United match, they struggled to be effective in the last third. Rico was again at his best delivering crosses, but the team couldn't get a clear chance from any of them. Solanke had the best chance first half but couldn't beat Tim Krul, who closed him down. Callum Wilson came close in the second half when Rico floated a ball in that the striker glided just wide with an outstretched foot. But it was Norwich who could have won it second half when Teemu Pukki shot from the edge of the box to have Ramsdale tipping it around the corner at full stretch.

'It is days like this when you have to come away and just be thankful that your team didn't lose the game. It could so easily have happened, as Norwich grew in confidence second half. While Eddie Howe must be pleased with a clean sheet, that is no goals scored in the last two matches and for those saying Fraser should start, it didn't make a dramatic difference to chances created,' I added.

Picking apart the match analysis meant focussing

on Bournemouth's attack who had failed to score. 'While Norwich are not the strongest of teams, they did test the Cherries with their 10 shots, even if they only managed one on target. Bournemouth will need to do better themselves in front of goal too with just 11 shots at home and two on target. There will be better days but at least Bournemouth took a point, which keeps them moving forward after the defeat against Arsenal,' I reported.

The team went out without Josh King, but were a credible attacking force, so why did Bournemouth fail to register many significant chances against Norwich City?

Firstly, you have to credit the visitors that grew into the game and commanded a slightly higher share of possession. Bournemouth didn't use the ball well enough in the areas where it mattered. The only player for me that looked to quicken things when AFCB got in and around the box was Diego Rico. Most of the time he looked up first before trying to cross or pass, but there were one or two occasions when he lost possession, just hoping that a quick pass would find a red and black shirt. I say that, and for me, Rico was the best Cherries player on Saturday.

'What I am saying is, why weren't Ryan Fraser and Harry Wilson more effective on the wings in getting past their markers and finding gaps amongst Norwich's midfield and defence? It was no surprise that Danjuma was given a chance and we saw from him some of the attacking mentality that I felt was missing from the earlier play.

'I am not sure if Bournemouth were looking to be too precise. They had worked their way through the defence on a couple of occasions but didn't finish well - yes, Solanke's chance stands out. Callum Wilson's foot out to try and direct the ball goalwards in the second half from Rico was just great improvisation. Sadly, it didn't quite come off. I didn't get the sense that Bournemouth got up a head of steam like they sometimes do.'

It was noticeable that Bournemouth had allowed Jefferson Lerma to rest up after the international break and his long-distance travelling. So, I was pondered if the Philip Billing and Lewis Cook partnership did enough in the Norwich game? 'Both Lewis and Philip would have known that they needed a big performance to hold on to their places next week, but I'm not sure they did enough to both remain in the team.

'Lewis Cook was certainly playing deeper than how I like to see him when he is in the team. Lerma does that job well and it complements Lewis when he can be the player further forward in central midfield. Lewis's great quality is in slipping balls down either side of central defenders for the runs of Callum or Solanke. He does his work at pace and is usually one step ahead. But playing a more defensive role doesn't always get the best out of his game.

# THE GOLALLESS MONTH                          81

'I also tend to think Philip Billing is great one week and then slightly disappointing the next. I don't know if it is his long stride that makes it look like he doesn't quite get to players quickly enough to make the challenge. He also looks like he is simply jogging alongside players, rather than hounding and forcing errors of the opposition. I know he can do it because we have seen it in some games when he shows a really strong appetite to get the ball off the opposition,' I added.

Playing bottom of the table Watford next, who hadn't won a game all season, might be just the match to see Bournemouth scoring a few goals I thought. But football doesn't work out as you'd hope on paper.

'Bournemouth failed to score for their third match in a row. Away at the bottom team, they had their chances, but a miss from Danjuma on his first start was the closest Bournemouth got. Steve Cook and Harry Wilson also hit the woodwork, but Bournemouth were sluggish in possession and had Aaron Ramsdale and Steve Cook, especially, to thank for the clean sheet.

'AFC Bournemouth made a couple of changes with Danjuma, King and Lerma coming into the starting 11 and Solanke, Harry Wilson and Lewis Cook making way for them.'

It was another match report that could only dwell on missed opportunities. 'The conditions didn't help matters but either side could have won this one and the biggest positive for Howe is a clean sheet. Bournemouth has gone three games now without scoring, which is not like them, and it was sad to see Callum Wilson not go the full 90 minutes. Steve Cook's header that hit the bar, Danjuma's shot that didn't go in from the six-yard box, Rico's volley and Harry Wilson's free kick - there were plenty of chances to score. Watford had chances too, but away to the bottom team, Bournemouth will be perhaps thinking this is two points dropped,' I said.

*Cherry Chimes'* next post on 28 October had a predictable headline – Are AFCB the new draw specialists? The month had seen Bournemouth fail to get a win and I was worried that it was becoming a habit. 'It hasn't been a highly memorable month in October for the Cherries. The two goalless draws against Norwich and Watford have slowed the momentum after the great wins against Everton and Southampton, and yet the Cherries are still sitting in the top 10.

'All the clubs are finding points hard to come by, if they are not in the top six. While Bournemouth has struggled to find form, that can also be said for clubs like Everton, Man Utd, Spurs and Watford, who have traditionally finished higher than AFCB. The annoying thing about the two recent draws AFCB have had is that they have had chances to win those games. The goals have dried up at both ends. While that is good from the defence, AFCB is lacking something in the final third.

'How Bournemouth could do with David Brooks returning. We may have to wait a bit longer yet. But not being able to beat the bottom team was perhaps a blow for the team. You could hear it in Adam Smith's post-match interview, he expected better. The conditions at Vicarage Road were not conducive for great football and neither team was able to get a real grip of the game, so I don't think a draw was unfair.'

I also felt sad for Aaron Danjuma, who had been given his first start and had been subbed, after missing a great chance. My thoughts went over to what Danjuma must have been thinking as he stepped off the field on Saturday to be replaced by Harry Wilson. 'He had just completed his first start for his new club and knew that he could have been a match-winner if he had just reacted better when Josh King had laid on an exquisite pass for him, across the box, that he would surely normally have knocked in.

'The day started brightly enough at Watford for Danjuma. He was perhaps criticised a little by Jason Tindall for not getting back and helping out Diego Rico enough, but Roberto Pereyra was causing problems all afternoon for Bournemouth, and all the players were wondering where he would pop up next.

'Once Danjuma had got his passing better, he did get into some great positions, and there was no better one than at the end of that first half, when he looked certain to score. It looked like he had made up his mind early to keep the shot low, as Foster came rushing out. It was a shame, as if he had lifted his head and just chipped the ball, he probably would have given AFCB a half-time lead.'

The month was drawing to a close, but there hadn't been a single goal in the three matches in October. All we could do is ask when would Bournemouth hit their top form?

'It has been hard to watch the Cherries of late. It is not that they haven't been trying, but they have looked nervous and fragile when they don't want to do the wrong thing. It may just be holding the players back. They need to play without fear and to go at teams, if they are to play at their best.

'We have been waiting for the Cherries to hit top gear for a few weeks now. It's not been happening. I don't see it being down to any one player in particular, but more of a team focus thing. Eddie may have switched the players' minds to a clean sheet mentality, which previously been hard to come by. Now the team seems to have lost something going forward. There is a switch that needs to be flicked somewhere but finding it is eluding Eddie Howe at the moment.

'I don't see the players getting the ball forward as quickly as we know they can. By slowing things down, they tend to be less sure of their passing. It is when

# THE GOLALLESS MONTH

stretching the opposition that AFCB always play at their best. The speed of Fraser and Adam Smith was certainly there on Saturday against Watford, but they couldn't deliver the quality crosses to cause real mayhem in Watford's defence.

'The way King delivered his cross for Danjuma's chance though may make Howe reconsider where Josh King plays next time. It was pin-point and getting the best out of Josh King is certainly needed to get AFCB firing.

'Callum Wilson cut a more puzzling figure to me when he was subbed for Dominic Solanke. He just hadn't seen as much ball as he would have liked, and more importantly, not in the areas where he could do any damage to the opposition. I can't see Callum being dropped from a starting spot, but Eddie Howe must be running out of ideas as to what he can do to get the forwards in more of a goal-scoring mood.'

There was no surprise where the player of the month award would go with three clean sheets and a month of no goals. Aaron Ramsdale could be pleased to pick up the award and look to try and beat Artur Boruc's AFC Bournemouth's Premier League record of nine clean sheets from 2016-17.

# Chapter 5. November – United, they fall

I wasn't overly confident that Bournemouth would do well against a resurgent Manchester United at the start of November. The Red Devils had come off a busy week, having beaten Norwich City 1-3 away from home, before beating Chelsea 1-2 away, at Stamford Bridge, in the Carabao Cup.

Meanwhile, Bournemouth hadn't scored in their last three games. They weren't starting matches well and the only improvement that we had seen was that they had stopped conceding goals, so the clean sheets were coming if not the wins.

Nothing seemed that glamourous about the Premier League when it was pouring down with rain at Dean Court and blowing a gale for the visit of Manchester United. The build-up to the game had been a bit strange for me as well, as it was an early 12:30 kick-off and I had lots on my mind.

I had been busy driving down from Redhill to see Paul Orchard at *In off the Far Post*. He had ordered some copies of *Eddie Had A Dream*, my first book, to sell in his shop in Pokesdown. I had managed to get down for 10 am and waited in the shelter of Paul's shop and took the opportunity to see England take on South Africa in the Rugby Union World Cup Final. It didn't go well for Eddie Jones' team, and I hoped that our Eddie would be more successful and perhaps get a draw in the afternoon.

But I felt more confident that the day could improve when I met up with Sam Davis, of the *Back of the Net* podcast, in the 1910 Bar. We had a quick conversation about *Eddie Had A Dream*, which we had an interview about the week before, on Sam's podcast, and agreed to meet up at half-time to do another quick interview that would go out later in the week. This one would update listeners on the progress of the book's sales.

Having exited the 1910 Bar, I spotting a past favourite walking into the stadium. It was Sylvain Distin. He was casually striding up to the stadium with nobody else approaching him. So, I stepped right up and asked him to sign a copy of *the Eddie Had A Dream* book, which he kindly did. I was over the moon, as Sylvain was only at the club for the first Premier League season for AFC Bournemouth, and I hadn't managed to get his signature before.

Armed with my signed copy, I felt that perhaps the luck was changing, even if the rain hadn't stopped. The match went pretty quickly in the first half. United should have scored early on, when their young Welsh attacker, Daniel James, crossed from the right straight into Andreas Pereira's stride. Pereira had the goal at his mercy, near the penalty spot, but the striker completely missed the ball and the danger passed.

The biggest turning point of the half perhaps came, not when Ryan Fraser went over in the box and VAR was called into play, but rather when Martial went down with Lerma in close attendance in Bournemouth's box. All hell let loose with accusations of diving and Fred getting more than a bit involved, pushing Lerma, who needed Aaron Ramsdale to help shepherd the Colombian away from the incident. It was too late for Lerma, who was booked and would be suspended for the next game. At least he didn't do anything more serious in retaliation.

Once rattled though, Bournemouth upped their game. The defining moment of the match came right on half-time. I was speaking into my voice recorder on my phone at the time, summing up the first half, when Adam Smith put in a high ball that Josh King chested down. Josh King allowed the ball to bounce before accepting the challenge from Aaron Wan-Bissaka and swivelled to his left to fire an unstoppable shot down and past David de Gea in goal. Like most Bournemouth fans, I didn't wait to hear a VAR check. I was pumping the air and shouting, 'King has scored! Josh has scored!' Bournemouth now had United just where they wanted them.

I duly did my half-time interview with *Back of the Net* and admitted that I'd got the score wrong – it wouldn't be a 0-0 result. But I hung on to the hope that the Cherries would keep their clean sheet and end the game 1-0, which is exactly what happened.

I summed up the match on the blog, feeling rather jubilant. 'In the end, the 1-0 win is pleasing in that Bournemouth took their best chance and kept United at bay for another clean sheet. Eddie Howe won't have much to grumble at after that performance, and the home crowd got fully behind the team which made it a great game to be at.'

Beating one United was fantastic, but could the Cherries do it twice? Well, the happy mood wouldn't last long. Bournemouth had to make their longest journey of the season for the next game up to Newcastle. While the Toon had not picked up that many points, they had beaten West Ham United in their last match and had beaten Man United just like Bournemouth. The Cherries had not lost against a team below them in the league up to this stage, so there was every reason to believe Bournemouth would return from St James' Park with something.

Before the game, I spoke with the *Newcastle United FC Blog* and had the following to say on Bournemouth's prospects.

NUFCB: Firstly, what sort of shape do you feel Bournemouth are in, coming into this one? Interested to know the feeling around the club and the general mood of fans 11 games into the new season.

CC: The fans are in a fairly good mood. We had a slightly disappointing start, with two newly-promoted clubs to face first up, but wins against Everton and Southampton were a timely boost. October was low on points as we drew most games, but at least we have started to get some clean sheets – three in a row now. The win against Man Utd last weekend has given us a good position in the league, but there have been a few points that have been squandered.

NUFCB: What are the strengths and weaknesses of this Bournemouth side, both individually and as a team? Give us some players to watch and weak links we could exploit.

CC: Of late, it has been the defence that has excelled. Diego Rico at left-back has been revitalised having hardly had a game last season. He is a great crosser of the ball and a great supply route for the strikers. In goal, Aaron Ramsdale has also been a class act, making some impressive saves.

The team will become very confident if it gets a goal up. The attacking play has been inconsistent though. The team can start slow, and then over-think things. They get frustrated quickly when they choose the wrong passes around the box. The ball over the top has also been a weakness this season, but Steve Cook and Nathan Aké are working hard to be as solid as they can at the heart of the defence.

NUFCB: What's the Bournemouth XI (and formation) likely to start on Saturday?

CC: I'd say it will be 4-4-1-1
Bournemouth has reverted to its old formation. They have been undone when not playing their familiar formation.

                    Ramsdale
        A Smith   S Cook   Aké   Rico
        H Wilson   L Cook   Billing   Fraser
                    King
                  C Wilson

NUFCB: What do you make of this Newcastle side and which players do you see as the strengths and weaknesses in our team?

CC: I haven't put Newcastle among the relegation teams this season. They look like a more formidable team and they have played well against the top teams, often only conceding a single goal. Allan Saint-Maximin looks an exciting player, and perhaps rather unpredictable. I like Jamaal Lascelles, at the back, who is calm as a defender and probably deserves more recognition than he gets. I have not seen much of Joelinton, so I'll be look to see how well he plays up-front.

Newcastle start games well but throw away some daft goals usually. Against Bournemouth, we have had some close games and I expect this to be the same and very end-to-end. It is taking their chances where I think Newcastle sometimes let themselves down. If they can start getting that right they will win many more points at home.

NUFCB: What sort of game do you think it'll be and how do you see it panning out? Give us a prediction.

CC: I mentioned that I think it will be end-to-end and quite frantic. Both teams know they can win this game and it will be a matter of who can impose themselves the best as always. Bournemouth has picked up points away from home in some games, so they won't be daunted by the big ground and noisy fans. But they know Newcastle United are in form. I just hope Bournemouth don't start too cautiously, which has been a trend of late.

I hope Bournemouth can win it 1-2, but I get the feeling it is more likely to be something like 3-3.

NUFCB: Which three sides do you see going down this season and why?

CC: My prediction at the start of the season was:
18 Sheffield Utd
19 Brighton
20 Aston Villa

So, I don't think we are on course for that now. Villa may still struggle as they have not got a squad with great depth - a few injuries and they'll be bang in trouble. You have to wonder if Watford can start putting some wins together and I think they will. The teams that I see being dragged into it now are Southampton and Norwich City. Norwich and Southampton are just conceding too many goals and you can see it continuing that way. So, Villa, Norwich and Saints may be playing in the Championship next season.

NUFCB: If you could sign one player from NUFC, who would you like to see Howe go for?

CC: Romantically, I should say Matt Ritchie but we are full of wingers. But I'll pick Jamaal Lascelles as our defence can always do with more height and a bit of ability on the ball.

NUFCB: Finally, if you had our two squads to

choose from and were asked to pick the best possible side, what would your starting 11 be?

CC:

> Ramsdale
> A Smith, Lascelles, Aké Clark
> Willems, Lerma, Shelvey, Fraser
> Saint-Maxim, C Wilson

With NUFC Blog sorted, it was time to shout 'away the lads, at the Toon!' Jefferson Lerma was suspended for the game after picking up his fifth yellow card and Lewis Cook took his place, while Dan Gosling returned to the bench, after his long-term injury had healed. Eddie Howe couldn't have wished for a much better start with a set-piece move from a corner. Ryan Fraser played it short to Josh King at the near post, before flicking a quick pass to around the penalty spot, where Harry Wilson had run, having bent his run from the far post. Harry shot low and past the Newcastle defender, into the bottom left corner of the net, and Bournemouth had their lead.

Possession was pretty much all Bournemouth at this stage and the points looked like they would be heading south, until the end of the first half when Allan Saint-Maximin sent in a cross to the far post and DeAndre Yedlin timed his run to perfection to make a diving header that levelled the scoring.

Newcastle United's crowd got behind their team

now A corner in the second half would undo the Cherries again when Ciaran Clark tapped in from close range. Aaron Ramsdale was by far Bournemouth's best player in making a stunning save at the feet of Saint-Maximin when he was through on goal. But the moment that will live with Bournemouth fans was the missed header by Josh King at the far post in added time. It was a sickener.

Bournemouth slipped down the league to ninth-position as they headed into the international break. Yet, again they had lost their last game before a two-week break and would need to refocus for the next part of the campaign.

Ryan Fraser wasn't given much time to reflect on his last game as *TalkSport* had him linked to advanced transfer talks with Liverpool for a January move. It was a rumour quickly denounced by the *Bournemouth Echo*. However, I wouldn't have been surprised though, if Liverpool were interested in the winger.

On 12 November, I posted on the rumours and what it might mean for Ryan to join such a club as Liverpool, which had an association with top Scottish players in its history.

'I am sure Andrew Robertson at Liverpool has been telling Ryan that he should come and join them and Liverpool has always had a strong bond with Scottish players in the past. Who wouldn't want to follow in the footsteps of Graham Souness and Kenny Dalglish?

'It won't be easy for Ryan to push into the starting 11, but I don't think that will bother him too much at Anfield. He'll have everything he needs around him to make him an even better player and Jurgen Klopp will be rubbing his hands to get hold of a player that has shown that he has great Premier League ability,' I said.

Another winger was also attracting some headlines for perhaps losing his direction. Jordon Ibe was to make a court appearance in November because he was accused of crashing his Bentley into a coffee shop in Bromley during the summer. Jordon Ibe's football career had similarly steered itself off course, having not played a game for the Cherries in the Premier League so far this season. Harry Wilson had breezed past him as first-pick for the right-wing and fans could expect Ibe to drive to another club come January.

If things seemed to be going wrong off the field for Bournemouth players, they weren't exactly going any better for former Cherry Carl Fletcher, who had left the club to join Leyton Orient as Head coach. Sadly, Carl lost his job in less than a month after five defeats and an FA Cup loss to eighth tier Maldon & Tiptree.

My promotion of *Eddie Had A Dream* was now in full swing. I had already done some prize competitions with *The Sack Race* and the *Back of The Net podcast,* and now I had the chance to go up to London to have a 15-minute radio broadcast with Paul Hawksbee and Andy Jacobs on their afternoon show for *TalkSport*. I had been on *TalkSport* a few times before, but they had since moved to their swanky new offices in London Bridge and I knew that the view was going to be great from the 22$^{nd}$ floor. I was nervous about what I might be asked. I knew I had to get a few points across no matter what, such as *Julia's House Children's Hospice* which would receive 15 per cent of every book sold. I also wanted to be clear that I wanted to express what it was like to be an AFC Bournemouth supporter and to mention that the book covered Eddie Howe's early playing years and the period he managed at Burnley.

The whole book launch process was completely new to me. I was doing a lot of things by trial and error, but I knew that having contacts in the right places was a great help. My previous work with *TalkSport* came up trumps there.

Just before my appearance on the radio, I decided to trek down to Ashley Heath, near Wimborne, as they were continuing to carry out car boot sales in November and into December. The Christmas Fairs were pretty much fully-booked, but my book launch had been at a great time when fans were looking to buy presents and receive gifts for Christmas. I thought there was no harm in taking a car-load of books down to the Bournemouth area and seeing if I could quickly sell out in a winter field. What was I thinking? I had to drive down from Surrey and the car boot sale, which was freezing, and started from 6.30 am! Still, my endeavours were appreciated as local people immediately recognised the AFC Bournemouth blanket on my table and came over to see what *Eddie Had A Dream* was all about.

I enjoy this kind of contact with people more than anything, as it puts me right next to fellow fans who are just as thrilled as me to talk about the Cherries.

Visiting *TalkSport* on 18 November was an altogether different experience, I hadn't been to their new studios before at London Bridge, but it is a glass building located directly outside London Bridge Station. You can't help but notice that this is where celebrities hang out as they promote their latest concert, book, or record. I felt like a bit of an imposter with pop group *Westlife* standing in the reception just before I went into the building.

Highlighting the cause of AFC Bournemouth can take me to some amazing places and meeting radio presenters is all part of the job. I was taken through security and past the back-lit, 6ft tall, panels with *News Corporation's Sun Newspaper* front pages and up to the 17th floor, where there was a green room awaiting me, just 20 minutes before going on air.

The room was spartanly decorated with a coffee machine and two sofas with a couple of *TalkSport* cushions for company. The white walls were decorated with a Chelsea shirt of Jason Cundy and an Ipswich shirt of Alan Brazil, while in between was a banner saying "It's not enough just to appear... You have to perform!"

Well, I had an idea of some things I wanted to say but you can't ever know what is going to come out when you are posed a question live on a national radio station.

I shook hands with Max Rushden, who was filling in for Paul Hawksbee, and also reached across to say hello to the bearded Andy Jacobs. Having presented them each with a copy of *Eddie Had A Dream*, it was time to go live on air. Max led the interview with some simple questions about why I would want to write the book. I eased into the interview with no real dramas.

I felt that the conversation was being directed to whether Eddie Howe should look to move away from the Cherries now, and the fact that Pochettino at Spurs was about to be fired the next day had something to do with it. But I explained there was a very special relationship between AFC Bournemouth and Eddie Howe and that the only job that might give him second thoughts was that of the England manager.

While the conversation continued with Max saying Eddie Howe is hardly a party animal, so was it hard to write the book? I felt like I was soon defending Eddie as if he wasn't seen as the typical topflight manager. I just hoped people listening would realise that I wrote the book to get across what a wonderful experience it is to follow Eddie Howe and the Cherries. It has certainly taken my life in a whole new direction.

I hadn't finished with my interviews on 18 November either. Straight after the broadcast with *TalkSport,* I had to race home for a chat with Josephine, a *Bournemouth University* student who wanted to ask me about AFC Bournemouth in the community and how it might have changed in the last few decades. I was quizzed about whether the club was the same with how it worked with the fans and what might have changed since it had become a Premier League club?

I explained that I didn't think the club's policy or intent had changed, but that the sheer nature of being a Premier League club meant that some things had altered. It is a bigger club now and dealing with things on a global scale when it came to the brand and everyday decisions. It still does everything it can to get out in the local community and interact with people and support good causes, but I suspected that many fans may feel as I do, in that the club has had to change to some extent in what it prioritises and how it spends its time with so many requests.

Of course, it is watching the games that are the biggest thrill about being a Bournemouth fan. The international break was finally over and

Bournemouth again had the chance of going top five if they could overcome Wolves at Dean Court. Eddie's pre-match press conference was initially focused on asking questions about the new incumbent at Spurs. José Mourinho had stepped back into management and would be facing the Cherries in his first home match, after playing West Ham United away. Eddie just said it was great for the league that José was back and that, while it was not ideal timing for Bournemouth to go to Tottenham, the club would relish the opportunity.

While the international break was in full-swing, I tracked Jefferson Lerma, Josh King, Chris Mepham, and Harry Wilson playing for their respective countries. Meanwhile, Aaron Ramsdale had an England U21 team match, and I had my appointment with the *Guardian* and *Observer*. They were asking bloggers to write a season update report and I gave the following answers on AFC Bournemouth.

**Best performance?** The away win at Southampton. Accomplished, and our first win at St Mary's – long overdue!

**And the worst?** Arsenal away: flatter than a can of coke left out overnight. We took too long to get going – a familiar problem this season.

**Happy with the manager?** Of course. If his team could defend better we might have lost him to a rival by now.

**Why I love … Jefferson Lerma** Not the quickest or the cleanest of players, but he just desperately wants to win. He's the heartbeat of the side.

**What is "the Bournemouth way"?** Under Eddie, it's about playing out from the back and sucking teams in. He likes counter-attacking, expressive players.

**Which figure from the past would you most want to bring back now?** Nigel Spackman had a great career here in the early 80s (119 games) and went on to play for Chelsea, Liverpool and Rangers. We could do with his pinpoint passing.

**How are you feeling about VAR?** Put it in the bin. Technology can't judge issues that just aren't black or white. A fiasco.

**Funniest moment so far …** Southampton's comic defending for our third goal: Angus Gunn and Jan Bednarek running into each other. Oh, and a certain 9-0 reverse to Leicester.

But it was Wolves who were the club most on Eddie's mind and that of his own players. Josh King was out with a hamstring strain, having played for Norway in the international break. David Brooks was still not fully training on the grass and Ryan Fraser faced a late fitness test before the game. Ryan Fraser had given the impression that things hadn't been the same at the Cherries since Marc Pugh had left to join QPR, but Eddie confirmed the winger had other players he got on well with.

Consistency was what Howe wanted to see and the Newcastle game had been a missed opportunity. Bournemouth had not been getting over the line in some matches but had created good moments against Newcastle and not taken them which was frustrating.

Eddie Howe also remarked on Carl Fletcher's difficult spell having left Bournemouth to manage again at Leyton Orient, but losing his job in under a month. Eddie said he would talk with Carl to see if he wanted to come back.

Regarding the current players in the squad, Jefferson Lerma was highlighted as having been a highly motivated player and being easy for Eddie to manage. Value for money? 'Yeah, I think so said Eddie, 'I think he's been really, really important. I think how you see him on the pitch is how you see him day-today – fully committed, wholehearted, very consistent, wants to win everything in training. And whatever you ask him to do he commits to it. I've got a lot of time for Jefferson, because of his mentality and how he conducts himself. He's very low maintenance from my side,' added Howe.

Eddie admitted that the side had been in with the chance of winning more games this season than in the past, without hitting the very best levels. He took that as a great sign because if they could find that extra five per cent the team will do well. But the more games you feel you should win and don't builds frustration and maybe confidence gets hit.

Playing Wolves would be hard but Eddie hoped he could get the home fans involved in the game. He made one change to the starting line-up, as Josh King had come back from international duty with Norway with a strained hamstring. Eddie decided to go with three centre-backs. Simon Francis was brought into the starting 11 and would captain the side. Sadly, it was not the return that Francis had hoped for.

With 20 minutes having gone, Francis slid into a challenge on Jota on the side of the penalty box and was yellow carded. Even worse, a minute later, João Moutinho slotted in the free kick to give Wolves the lead. Francis's problems weren't over though. A second yellow card followed on 37 minutes when he pulled a Wolves shirt in the box and was spotted making the foul by the referee. What a comeback! I just wondered if Eddie Howe had misjudged whether Francis had been given enough high-class games before his return to the first team. It had all gone horribly wrong.

At 0-2 down on 45 minutes, Bournemouth needed an amazing half-time talk. Whether Eddie was angry or restored confidence in underperforming players, the second half would be different.

Switching to a 4-4-1 formation, Eddie Howe subbed Harry Wilson and Philip Billing at the interval. This allowed Arnaud Danjuma and Jefferson Lerma to come on and they made a big difference. Suddenly the crowd had been re-incentivised and got behind the team as they came forward. The breakthrough came from a corner, when Steve Cook rose at the near post and headed a glancing blow that saw the ball nestle inside the far post 1-2!

Was an unthinkable comeback on? Bournemouth kept trying and a goalmouth scramble with Steve Cook and Nathan Aké having shots blocked had us standing up expectantly. But the big chance came right at the end in added time when Steve Cook won a header. Callum Wilson gained control and squared the ball to the on-rushing Danjuma who sliced his shot horribly wide. It was game over and no points for the Cherries.

Eddie had to talk to the press post-game and he summed up his regret at how he set the team up. 'I thought we could have been braver with and without the ball. ...The supporters were brilliant and I felt for them watching the first half. I was doing the same and it wasn't good to watch,' said Eddie Howe.

In the following week, I had plenty of time to

reflect on the Wolves game. I had to start with Simon Francis' sending off. Was time running out on his playing career at this level?

'Simon Francis has some serious thinking to do. He will be devastated about his last match. It should have been a great return for the captain and yet he was out of touch and unable to cope with the pace of Wolves' attack. Jota had his number and Simon will be frustrated that he didn't do better,' I wrote.

While defenders are always going to make the odd mistake, it was a risk to bring back Simon Francis into the set-up that had been doing well as a back four. The balance just didn't work with Simon trying to fit in and seal up the right side. While Eddie believes he picked the right man for the job, Francis has been out for a long time and perhaps hasn't been tested enough before making this return against such a quick attack.

I couldn't hide my disappointment on the blog. 'Just when you hope that Bournemouth has taken a lesson from their game before the international break, we were served up an indifferent first half against Wolves, and an experienced captain was left holding his head in his hands after making a couple of mistakes,' I said.

The game very quickly went away from the Cherries because they didn't concentrate on two set-pieces, and they let their guard down at really important times.

The next question was why were Bournemouth better when they went down to 10-men? Eddie Howe couldn't explain why Bournemouth showed more spirit and fight when going down to 10-men. Yes, he had told the players that they were playing for the fans and their families in the second half to make sure the score was not embarrassing, but something was yet again wrong about the mentality in the first 45 minutes and it's not the first time we have seen it this season.

Wolves didn't open Bournemouth up the whole game. They were prepared to shoot from outside the box and perhaps wouldn't have been such a problem had they not been given free kick opportunities. "Two set-pieces were the open door that Wolves needed to win the game. It must be agonisingly annoying for Eddie Howe when the team can't defend properly at such moments. The team has the opportunity to get ready and be prepared for the free kicks when they come in, but Bournemouth just didn't have all the bases covered and they looked extremely vulnerable when Wolves had free kicks.

Ramsdale didn't get off the ground quickly enough for Moutinho's goal. Why that was I'm not sure. Perhaps he didn't think the shot would be direct and expected it to be a cross. But he was caught out by a marvellous shot. Moutinho probably put it in the only small space that he could to beat Ramsdale. It was hit very high and had a very sharp dip on it.

'Less forgivable was the second goal. The ball between Harry Wilson and Lewis Cook was expertly played, but Bournemouth were caught on the back foot. Once the cross from Adama Traore was put right in front of Raul Jimenez, it was simple for the striker to score, having got ahead of Nathan Aké.'

All would be forgiven if Bournemouth could get a result against Tottenham. I was unable to go to the match because I had hoped there would still be some tickets left by the time the point system fell low enough for my boys to come along. Sadly, we missed out. My first visit to Tottenham's new stadium would have been special, but my friends, Damien Hill and Michael Dunne ensured I'd have some pictures for the blog and I could stream the game at home.

The line-up for Bournemouth was a bit of a shock as Adam Smith was ill and did not travel, which meant Jack Stacey had a start at right-back. Arnaut Danjuma was preferred to Harry Wilson and with Josh King out, Dominic Solanke had brushed off his hamstring problems to make a start.

While Bournemouth started to play very well in the early moments with lots of possession, there was always a nagging doubt that Spurs might create something at any moment. Sure enough, they did. A long pass up the middle of the pitch by Toby Alderweireld undid the Cherries back four and Dele Alli was left to stride through and score the opening goal. Worst still, a carbon copy replica at the start of the second half made it 2-0, before a swift attack by Spurs, down the left-wing, saw Moussa Sissoko volley a cross into the back of Bournemouth's net to make it 3-0 on 69 minutes.

Bournemouth had been out-played and I was glad that I hadn't been able to get a ticket. I still had memories of the 5-0 defeat up at Wembley the previous season, when Simon Francis had picked up a cruciate ligament injury. At least there were no injuries this time, but what we hadn't had in that game was a sub who could change the direction of the game. This time Harry Wilson came on and started to impress very quickly. His first major contribution was a free kick, which he curled over the wall and into the top right corner to make it 3-1 with 17 minutes to go.

While Bournemouth couldn't find another opening until added time. Harry Wilson was then on cue again to make it 3-2, on 90+6 minutes. We all thought that was it, but there was a golden opportunity for Callum Wilson and Harry Wilson to get the equaliser from a long ball up-field. The two seemed to let the ball bounce and Callum was favourite to get his strike away, but Toby Alderweireld rushed in to stop the shot and the chance was gone.

A 3-2 defeat didn't seem that terrible. At least Bournemouth had been able to claw some goals back. But with no points from their last three games, the situation was starting to get nervy. We knew there were some big teams to play in December and the good start had not been built on strongly enough in October and November.

# Chapter 6. December – It's a relegation fight

We wouldn't have too long to reflect on the defeat at Spurs. The games would come thick and fast in December. Before AFC Bournemouth had kicked another ball, they had been picked out of a black bag in the FA Cup by Micah Richards for a third round tie with Championship side Luton Town, who were drawn out by Tony Adams. The game would be played in January, so we had a home tie to look forwards to.

On a cold Tuesday evening, I met up with my two boys at Redhill station before travelling up to Selhurst Park for the next away game. We travelled up by train as it should have been easy, but a fire on the line made it a tight timescale to make kick-off. I was already wondering if I'd have been better to have watched the game on *Amazon Prime* like many others – it was their first live broadcast Premier League game. But over 1000 fans made a loud enough noise to let the players know we were there to support them on a chilly night.

The game itself saw Chris Mepham come in for Steve Cook, who had fractured his wrist in the Tottenham match. Philip Billing returned from his one-match suspension and Harry Wilson started on the right-wing, while Ryan Fraser sat on the bench.

Bournemouth began well with much of the ball. It looked like it would be a great night when Sakho was sent off for a sliding challenge on Adam Smith. But Bournemouth couldn't make the extra man count. Callum Wilson missed a great chance to score from a Harry Wilson cross, running right through the six-yard box, while Dominic Solanke missed his chance when trying to square a pass up for Callum, rather than shoot himself. The final insult came when Jeffrey Schlupp strode past, Solanke, Lerma and Chris Mepham to fire in Palace's winner in a game where they had hardly seen the ball.

Eddie Howe didn't hide away from the truth. He said he had to take responsibility for the team's performance, but couldn't understand why they hadn't performed well again. He even said it was probably as low as he has ever felt as Bournemouth manager in the Premier League. I don't know about the team needing a pick me up, it certainly seemed that Eddie needed to hear some good news. With most of the games being played on Wednesday night Bournemouth hung on to the hope that not too many teams around them would jump past them in the table. Bournemouth did remain in 12$^{th}$ spot after the

# IT'S A RELEGATION FIGHT

Wednesday night but sat just two points above the relegation zone.

I had driven down to Bournemouth that Wednesday to join with some 150 members of the AFC Business Community for the annual Christmas Lunch. The event gave me a chance to meet up with many local contacts and I was pleased to avoid the glaze of Jimmy Glass, AFC Bournemouth's Player Liaison Officer, who was dishing out the singing punishments for any guests that touched their phone during the quiz. He delighted in picking out a few offenders and I was sure he had plenty of practice at spotting minor misdemeanours with the players over the years.

Bournemouth's crimes on the pitch were certainly growing. I listened in to the *Back of the Net* podcast to get a feel of the current mood and reaction of the fans – it was damning of both the players and the nonsensical substitutions Eddie was making. Everyone was trying to fathom out why the Cherries were playing such dire football.

Eddie gave several interviews saying that he was happy at the club and that the Everton job speculation is not something he paid attention to. But there was something not quite right in the dressing room. You could sense it. Was Callum Wilson sulking at Ryan Fraser's wish to leave in January, or at the end of the season? Did the return of Simon Francis cause tension in that his legs had seemed to have gone? Were the players frustrated, that David Brooks needed yet another month to recover from his ankle injury? It was probably a combination of things that were getting spirits down, but the season doesn't stop when you are having a bad run and, if things were said behind closed doors, we hoped it would have a reaction when Liverpool visited.

Liverpool was eight points clear of Leicester City at the top of the league and was racing away towards the Premier League title. What on earth could a down-trodden, injury-ridden, and out of form AFC Bournemouth side do against players at the top of their game?

Some bookies were still giving Bournemouth odds of 6-1 for an upset against Liverpool, despite the Merseysiders being unbeaten since the start of the season. Perhaps 600-1 would have been fairer odds? Still we travelled down to the game in anticipation of a better showing than the team had made against Crystal Palace, only a few days before.

Eddie Howe didn't have a lot of choice in terms of selection decisions. He made just one change with the injured Adam Smith being replaced by captain Simon Francis. It was hoped that Francis would last longer than he did in the last home game. The problem wouldn't be sending offs this time, it would be more injuries and this time to key players.

Bournemouth started the game brightly and was holding Liverpool with the first half-hour passing. It

# IT'S A RELEGATION FIGHT

was then that Mo Salah went on a strong diagonal run to receive a long pass into Bournemouth's box and Nathan Aké over-stretched to win the ball and make the tackle on Salah. The Dutchman couldn't carry on. It meant an opportunity for Jack Simpson. But while Simpson was getting ready, a long ball over the top picked out Alex Oxlade-Chamberlain and Chris Mepham hadn't initially seen the run. It was too late. The former Southampton player scored and Bournemouth were a goal down to the league leaders on 35 minutes.

There was obvious annoyance in Bournemouth's ranks. It was another long ball that had not been defended well. It was becoming a bad habit. Matters soon became worse when Mo Salah moved into the box and surrounded by Bournemouth players, still managed to slip a ball through to Naby Keïta to make it 0-2 to Liverpool on half-time.

With Everton winning at home to Chelsea, supporters knew Bournemouth would be slipping further down the table. Before the hour Salah had made it 0-3. If the home crowd were able to marvel at Liverpool's great play and try and forget what it was doing to Bournemouth's league position, it was a crushing blow when Callum Wilson pulled up with a hamstring problem.

Such was the scarcity of attacking options on the bench that Lewis Cook and Dan Gosling were the only players that Howe released in the second half from the bench. Jordon Ibe was probably still out of favour, having crashed his car and not having told the manager. Jordon would have probably loved to have had some minutes against his old club.

While the game ran out 0-3, AFCB fans could only wonder where the next win could come from. Some nine senior players were now injured and unavailable for selection. At least November's player of the month, Harry Wilson, would be available to play against Chelsea in the next match, not that Danjuma or Fraser had played that badly against Liverpool. Eddie Howe was concerned with the injuries and even more concerned that players were not getting back to fitness once being injured. Recurring injuries just kept happening. Howe said that the team would regroup, but it was not clear who he'd have available to regroup with for the next game with so many regular first-team players now out of action.

The league table was looking gloomy with Bournemouth now 15$^{th}$ and just one point above the relegation zone, after 16 matches, on a total of 16 points. Bournemouth's form was now the worst in the league with five defeats in a row.

All we needed to hear from *SkySports* was that Eddie Howe admitted he had no influence over whether Nathan Aké would remain a Bournemouth player for any amount of time. Aké's 2017 contract came with a buy-back option for Chelsea at £40m, giving the London club first option to buy him back.

# IT'S A RELEGATION FIGHT

With the January window coming into view, and Chelsea free of the UEFA transfer ban, Bournemouth fans suddenly saw that Nathan Aké might have already played his last game for the Cherries.

If the defence was going to be stretched, Eddie Howe would also need to rethink what he could do in attack against Chelsea. The hope was that Josh King might be able to start. I thought that even if King was only 90 per cent match fit, Howe would probably go with the former Blackburn attacker at Stamford Bridge. 'The good news is that Josh King has not been rushed back, but has been training and does not seem to have suffered any problems with his hamstring. If Josh can lead the line, then Bournemouth already looks stronger than they were in the second half against Liverpool, when Callum Wilson pulled up. It is funny that Josh King was complaining at the start of the season that he wanted to play through the middle. Well now he is likely to get his chance,' I said.

Eddie Howe confirmed in his pre-match press conference that Josh King was likely to be available for the Chelsea game, even though he had a small amount of training in the week. Still, he had trained well.

It's a real challenge to take on a team like Chelsea at any time, but with so many injured players it was hard to know exactly how Eddie Howe would attempt to get something from the game. But Bournemouth has a great record at Stamford Bridge and the Bournemouth players clearly enjoy playing there because this was one of the performances of the season.

Four changes were made to the team with Josh King leading the line and midfield being bolstered with Lewis Cook and Dan Gosling, while Jack Stacey came into the back four. Fans also gave a huge cheer out when the name of Junior Stanislas was read out among the substitutes. By just playing King up front and Ryan Fraser and Lewis Cook on the wings, Howe was looking to stop Chelsea and still hope that the midfield players could get up to help Josh.

The plan worked well first half, although Aaron Ramsdale was called upon to make an incredible block with a star-shaped save from Mason Mount early on. The Cherries had to do a lot of defending, but the back four held firm, with Mepham and Francis forming a good centre-back pairing.

While there were some hairy moments with a Stacey clearance that rocketed past Ramsdale and a Mepham interception that was headed goalwards, Ramsdale made the saves. Therefore, it was great to end the half, with Tammy Abrahams heading over and a scoreline of 0-0 remaining.

Considering that Bournemouth was on a five-game losing streak, a draw at this stage was more than what had been expected. But the second half was going to be a bigger test with Chelsea coming out

# IT'S A RELEGATION FIGHT

more anxiously to get a break through. The tackles kept going in though from Lerma and Gosling, and if the odd pass had been better Bournemouth could have got something on the break. King was coming into his own and Fraser was eager to get up in support.

With King being injured, he rolled off the pitch and Dominic Solanke came on to sub him. At this stage, Bournemouth fans were cheering their team on and hoping to hold out for a draw. Only Fraser's shot in the first few minutes had been on target. But there were similarities to the 2015 win that Bournemouth had at Stamford Bridge. The players were putting everything into the game and Dan Gosling found himself unattended, as the ball was fed back into the box. He had his back to goal, but instinctively tried a backward lob that went over Kepa's head and dipped under the bar. Is that a goal? Was he offside and did the defender get back in time to clear the ball before it crossed the line? Bournemouth fans shouted for VAR, while the referee waved play on at first.

But VAR was intervening – a goal check came up on the screen! Bournemouth fans waited and waited. The delay was extremely long, several minutes. The more we waited, the more I thought, they're going to give this to us. The ref's got it wrong. Indeed, Bournemouth was awarded a goal, and Gosling was soon jumping around and punching the air with delight while being mobbed by his team-mates. Bournemouth were winning the game and there were only five minutes left. This was really happening. Bournemouth tried to hold on for three points now, not one point. Fans were singing VAR, oh VAR! Referee, Graham Scott hadn't given Bournemouth much all game and had even given Chelsea goal kicks when they should have been Bournemouth corners. But now Bournemouth were in charge and marching towards victory. It had been a win against a team that had just qualified for the last 16 in the Champions League. Bournemouth had not only held them, they'd out-witted them.

The final match scenes were just great to be watching. The players were overjoyed at the support they had been given and were taking their shirts off to hand to the young fans. This was a huge three points that might only take Bournemouth up to 14th in the league, but it was a triumph for the players in adversity. They had come through an almost impossible test and won. If they could win at Stamford Bridge, they could win elsewhere and Eddie Howe knew it.

Howe spoke to *BBC Radio Solent* after the game and admitted he'd gone into the game with a plan. 'We needed to play a certain way today. We set up to frustrate them to give their centre-halves the ball but to try and protect our goal. I thought the back five, I include the goalkeeper in that, really stepped up today... As a team, I thought we were a real threat second half. That's why I think we just about shaded it.'

The win might not have meant that Bournemouth were safe, but the fact that they won when they were given no hope of getting anything mattered enormously. It was like a weight being lifted. The fans could enjoy the week ahead knowing that their team was back up and running.

Junior Stanislas was a bonus. He had been out since April 2019 and, as fans, we just hoped he could get more than a few games, as he always seemed to get injured. As a free kick specialist and an attacker, he boosted the squad at just the right time. We found out after the Chelsea match that Harry Wilson had missed the game, because he had a dead leg that was swelling up during training. Arnaut Danjuma had also picked up a foot injury, so Bournemouth were suddenly looking short of wingers.

The build-up to the Burnley home match would be a pleasing moment for Stanislas I thought, as it was one of his former clubs. He was probably banging on Eddie Howe's door begging him to play.

Burnley had only won one away game all season at bottom of the table Watford. It could be assumed that Burnley was struggling in these away games and it should be a good chance for Bournemouth to get a back-to-back win. Eddie Howe was just emphasising that the team had to remember the qualities that earned them the win against Chelsea and that some of those factors needed to be replicated more consistently if Bournemouth were to feature higher in the league table.

I was not so concerned about the defence after the Chelsea match. Aaron Ramsdale had been superb and was the subject of much chatter on *TalkSport* as Darren Gough was considering which England goalkeepers were in line for the Euros and he mentioned that Ramsdale was good but perhaps made mistakes as a young keeper. Pickford was the best England had he felt, but *Cherry Chimes* was among many Bournemouth fans asking what mistakes Ramsdale had made? And that Ramsadale had to be seen to be believed.

The centre-back pairing of Simon Francis and Chris Mepham also seemed to be working well. Chelsea was the first time I could recall that the two had started for Bournemouth in the centre-back positions together. Now they could perhaps go on a run and give Eddie Howe a problem when Aké and Steve Cook returned.

While analysing the Burnley stats pre-match, it was clear that they had scored more goals than Bournemouth with 22 to the Cherries' 19 goals from 17 games. Burnley also sat two places higher in 12$^{th}$, so we couldn't expect anything but a tough, physical game. Just what you need when you have a team that

# IT'S A RELEGATION FIGHT

is already patched up and stretched for available players.

The rain greeted fans to Dean Court on match day. There was plenty of Christmas cheer about on 21 December with AFCB Santa hats being given out and a festive *MatchDay* programme. Spirits didn't remain high for long though. It was a turgid first half with no shots on target, and it was incident-packed with free kicks. Simon Francis picked up a head injury from Ashley Barnes' boot and Ryan Fraser was left face down, looking at the turf on more than one occasion.

Bournemouth fans were annoyed at the referee, Martin Atkinson, who didn't want to use his yellow cards at first. But more animosity was saved for Ashley Barnes when he went down in the penalty box, before a corner. Philip Billing had swung around but hadn't touched him. The home crowd yelled, 'You are embarrassing!' to Barnes for the rest of the game until he was subbed. The game was so bad, there were also chants to the Burnley fans of 'How can you watch this every week?'

Burnley had come to make it as physically demanding as they could on Howe's injury ravished team. But Bournemouth couldn't create any chances. They defended well at the back for 88 minutes and then, a minute later, a cross found its way to substitute Jay Rodriguez who headed a winner. Burnley had done it again, spoilt Christmas and taken all three points!

It was left to a disappointed Howe to speak to the cameras and utter his dismay at how a team that he prides on its attacking desire couldn't manage a single shot on target. He admitted that the players had switched off in the last few minutes when Burnley had scored but felt the defence had otherwise dealt with the Burnley attacks well.

If the team had lacked creativity, Dominic Solanke and Callum Wilson hadn't made much difference second half. I was more surprised that Howe hadn't used Junior Stanislas who was also sitting on the bench. I wrote on *Cherry Chimes*, 'He was just what Bournemouth needed - fresh legs, creativity and a real goal threat. But Howe chose not to play him. Whether he wanted to protect him or didn't feel it was the right match for him, I'm not sure. But when the team lacks creativity, why leave one of the most creative players in the squad on the bench?

'I'd like to think that Junior was ready to play. He shouldn't be on the bench unless he is fit and ready. We know how good he is and what he can do, which made it all the stranger that Eddie didn't turn to him. Burnley was an old club of Junior's, and he would have busted a gut to do well against them.'

I was also of the feeling that Bournemouth had not played their own game against Burnley. They had got tangled up in the physical battle and hadn't stuck to their game by getting the ball down and getting their quick passing going.

# IT'S A RELEGATION FIGHT 127

While Callum Wilson had returned to play the second half of the Burnley game, Eddie Howe announced before the next game against Arsenal that he'd have perhaps just one more player back from injury. He didn't say who that could be the day before Christmas Eve, but I kind of prayed that it might be Lloyd Kelly if Howe wanted to play a back four. Diego Rico had been booked against Burnley, and it was his fifth card of the season, so an automatic one-match suspension. He'd miss the Boxing Day clash with Arsenal. My gut feeling was that Steve Cook might be the more likely candidate to make it back from injury, as he just needed a protective cast on his wrist to rejoin the action.

Arsenal themselves had not been on the best of runs having relieved temporary manager Freddie Ljungberg with a new permanent manager – Mikel Arteta. Arteta had left his position as number two at Man City and it would be his first game as a Premier League manager. It didn't make it easy for Howe to know how Arsenal would set up, but Arsenal was not having a great time of it. They were sitting 11$^{th}$ in the league with six points from their last five away games.

Bournemouth were hanging on in 14$^{th}$ place with just 19 points from 18 games, just four points more than Aston Villa in 18th. At least Bournemouth wouldn't be in the bottom three at Christmas, but the gap was small to the drop zone.

Steve Cook returned as captain for the Arsenal game with a cast over his injured left wrist. Jack Simpson also had a rare start as Diego Rico was suspended. Callum Wilson made a start having been a sub in the previous match. Harry Wilson returned to the bench, along with Philip Billing, who had some illness in the week, but Simon Francis was out because of a knee injury.

Arsenal came forward well against the Cherries with Saka finding it easy to get in behind on the left. Mesut Özil was also being given too much space, but it was Bournemouth who took the lead on 35 minutes when Dan Gosling got on the end of a Jack Stacey pull back. The Bournemouth press had worked well and Arsenal had failed to play out well from the back.

Josh King missed out on a great chance to extend the lead, just before half-time when he might have cut the ball back to a frustrated Callum Wilson rather than shoot from a narrow-angle himself. However, Bournemouth could be delighted to take a 1-0 lead into the break. The second half saw more rain tumble down as Pierre-Emerick Aubameyang went close with a curling shot just over the right upright. Steve Cook and Jack Stacey had to make heroic blocks to stop Özil and Aubameyang's shots.

Arsenal would not be denied though. Özil on the right passed to Maitland-Niles, who quickly moved the ball on to Aubameyang on the left. He squirted a shot past Ramsdale at the foot of the left post on 64 minutes. Right at the end of the game, Arsenal broke and Joe Willock had a chance to win the game, but he shot right at Ramsdale, who was pleased to make the save.

A 1-1 draw felt almost like a defeat but in the cold light of the next 24 hours, Bournemouth fans looked more favourably upon the result as a point taken from a usual top-six team. Bournemouth had fallen to 16$^{th}$ place in the league and were just two points above Aston Villa who were in 18$^{th}$ place. Any defeat would put Bournemouth in the bottom three. The next game would be against Brighton & Hove Albion, who were in 15$^{th}$ place, sitting just above Bournemouth on goals scored.

The good news for Bournemouth was that they had players coming back. Harry Wilson had come on as a sub against Arsenal, Callum Wilson had a game under his belt, although he now had five yellow cards and a suspension, and Steve Cook had returned. Diego Rico would also be available for the early 12.30 kick-off against Brighton for Bournemouth's last match of 2019 on 28 December.

Brighton & Hove Albion had only beaten Eddie Howe in the league once since December 2008 and Bournemouth certainly had the upper hand on history going into the match at the Amex Stadium. What nobody had countered on was the startling opening that Brighton had when their Iranian player, Alireza Jahanbakhsh, scored his first Premier League goal in the third minute.

It was an uphill battle from there on for Bournemouth. Eddie Howe had made five changes to the starting line up to rest Jefferson Lerma, Ryan Fraser, Callum Wilson and Lewis Cook. It hadn't worked. Dominic Solanke was still not finding a way to goal and Josh King spurned Bournemouth's best chance of the first half when Mathew Ryan got down well to save low to his left.

Just 1-0 down at half-time didn't seem so bad, but Brighton then had a VAR decision go against them when the ball bounced in Bournemouth's box before Dan Burn turned sharply to put the ball in the back of the net. VAR ruled offside from the initial free kick and Bournemouth thought they'd had a reprieve. But that didn't last long, because Aaron Moy chopped inside Chris Mepham, and fired past Aaron Ramsdale to make it 2-0 to Brighton on 79 minutes.

While Ryan Fraser and Callum Wilson tried to make a difference as second half subs, Bournemouth had been sunk. Junior Stanislas had made his first start since April 2019, but he didn't impact the game. Eddie Howe's job suddenly felt like it was under threat. All he could say was that it had been a 'tough, tough day.'

Bournemouth were in free fall. They now sat in 16th place and just two points above 18th placed Aston Villa in the relegation zone. The Cherries had only amassed 20 points from their first 20 games and

# IT'S A RELEGATION FIGHT 131

getting above the 40-point mark looked like it would be harder than ever. The immediate situation hadn't been helped by seeing Josh King and Jack Stacey pick up injuries against Brighton and they would now be likely to miss out on the next fixture in just three days.

# Chapter 7. January – Down but not out

If Bournemouth fans thought the Brighton & Hove Albion match was a must-win game, they did not doubt that the next fixture away to West Ham United was no less important. West Ham United had just sacked Manuel Pellegrini, after their 2-1 defeat to Leicester City and had quickly appointed David Moyes as their new manager. West Ham United was a place below the Cherries in 17th and just a point behind. A win for either team would pull them away from the relegation zone, so it was all set up for a relegation six-pointer, on 1 January 2020.

Everyone knew how important the game was, but with Aston Villa winning the early kick-off game, Bournemouth and West Ham had both dropped another place in the table. The Cherries brought Simon Francis in at right-back and Jefferson Lerma and Lewis Cook started in midfield, while Callum Wilson returned in attack. Junior Stanislas and Philip Billing were put on the bench, while Ryan Fraser had been ill and so was also on the bench. What we didn't know, at the time, is that several players were starting who Eddie Howe later admitted were carrying knocks and had not trained, like Steve Cook and Jefferson Lerma.

Looking at the players in the tunnel before kick-off, Simon Francis appeared nervous as he peered across at Mark Noble. West Ham's captain was focused with his eyes forward and in stark contrast to the fidgeting Simon Francis. A sign of things to come? Well, Bournemouth soon found themselves cursing their luck as Robert Snodgrass ran behind Diego Rico on the right-wing and pulled back a pass that Noble hit and deflected in, off Lewis Cook, to put the Hammers 1-0 up on 17 minutes.

While Bournemouth had a penalty shout for Harry Wilson going down in the box, it was dismissed by a VAR check. Fredericks then put in another cross from the right and Haller beat Steve Cook to the ball with an amazing volley that swung straight into the bottom left side of the goal – 2-0 to West Ham.

By the time we got to 35 minutes, it was 3-0 with Mark Noble perhaps clipping his own feet under pressure from Harry Wilson, but VAR not overruling the referee's decision for a penalty. Mark Noble had no trouble sending Aaron Ramsdale the wrong way and he had his second goal.

Bournemouth had to wait until the 41st minute before they could even get a strike on goal from Diego Rico. Eddie Howe reacted at half-time by subbing Diego Rico and Harry Wilson to bring on Ryan

Fraser and Junior Stanislas. If Bournemouth were hoping for a change in fortune, it didn't come. Anderson got in a foot race with Simon Francis and easily beat Bournemouth's right-back and slipped another goal past Ramsdale for 4-0 on 67 minutes.

While the game was lost, there was still the added indignity of Aaron Cresswell's sliding challenge on Ryan Fraser, initially given as a red card dismissal, only for VAR to overturn the decision and reduce it to a yellow card. Just to underline that it hadn't been Bournemouth's day, Ryan Fraser got back up and put in a perfect cross for Dominic Solanke in the last 10 minutes that Solanke headed against the far post and back into Fabiański's hands.

The defeat was humiliating and the recriminations would begin straight away by the fans who were distraught at knowing that Bournemouth had fallen into the bottom three and was now staring relegation in the face.

Bournemouth looked pitiful and the reality was that they had been playing badly for three months. Now they were looking up with most teams above them in the table. The players and the fans knew that if this form continued they would be playing Championship football next season.

I didn't find it easy to speak about the defeat to West Ham United on the blog. 'Bournemouth's players looked like lost lambs and they had no way of getting back into the game. We can look at bad luck in the first goal, but from there on in, there was nothing to suggest there was anything but another defeat on its way.

'To lose 4-0 away from home is bad at any time. To lose to the team below you in the table and to fall into the bottom three might be seen by some fans as a capitulation,' I commented.

Perhaps the Championship was beckoning for the Cherries. I was not giving up hope, but the team needed to find some inspiration from somewhere. 'Perhaps five years is a good run for a small team in the Premier League? If so, then we have had a good time, but it's hard to believe the club has gone through what it has to get to this position now. It is almost as if things are conspiring against AFCB and Eddie Howe with other teams winning when they had looked in real danger. Bournemouth now had to make sure they keep in touch with the clubs above them and that work has to start immediately. We have four immediate cup finals against the teams around us after next weekend. Then AFCB has a dog fight to try and stay up in March and April. If AFCB is not safe by May, it's likely to be bad news. Finding winnable games has never looked so hard as this.' I added.

Listening to all the comments from Bournemouth fans on social media was hard enough. Serious questions were being asked about whether Eddie Howe had done all he could for the Cherries. But how could we say goodbye to the man that had given the club everything it had enjoyed for the last decade? He really was Mr Irreplaceable to most of the fans, including myself.

I was turning my attention to the players and trying to work out why the team wasn't scoring anymore. The West Ham game was one where we would have thought we'd get a fair number of chances, but the creativity of the team had disappeared.

'Bournemouth are not only out of sorts, they don't have anyone who looks like they will score at the moment. Bournemouth toiled for 95 minutes against West Ham, but they only managed three shots and just two of them were on target. Callum Wilson wasn't even the player to have the shots and the best Dominic Solanke could do was hit the post from three yards,' I wrote on *Cherry Chimes*.

The prospect of the transfer window opening up in January didn't give fans much consolation, after Eddie Howe's comments that his main priority was to get the injured players back first and see how things were at the end of January with the squad.

I had no confidence that Bournemouth would bring any more than just the one loan player, and even then, it was hard to know who Bournemouth could pick up. 'The prospect of bringing a forward in on loan seems remote with Eddie suggesting it is hard in the January window. The message may well be that

AFCB can't afford to spend further, and if that means they have to go down to the Championship, perhaps it was a mistake to let Lys Mousset go. Other Premier League teams might be able to deal with such a big injury list as Bournemouth have, as they are bigger clubs with more payers of a high standard. If Bournemouth can't compete with those teams, then perhaps they are fighting above their true position and Howe was bound to be caught out at some point with a smaller squad,' I wrote.

Bournemouth just didn't have a big enough goal threat, Sam Surridge had to be recalled from his loan at Swansea City and signed a new four-and-a-half-year deal at Bournemouth. What Bournemouth needed was a saviour for this season. This was not about any future potential, Bournemouth needed a miracle now. Even if they were only one point off safety, things could get very bad, very quickly, with games against Watford, Norwich City, Brighton & Hove Albion and Aston Villa in the next four league games. All of them were six-pointer games!

Before those crucial league games, there would be the light relief of the FA Cup. Bournemouth had not had a good FA Cup run for a few seasons and being drawn against Luton Town, who were bottom of the Championship, should have given Bournemouth fans great hope of progression in a normal season. But with Eddie Howe expected to rest players for the Premier League fight to stay up, many fans wondered whether it would be a good thing to progress in the Cup. Maybe it was better to bow out now and save the energy for Premier League survival.

Eddie Howe selected a much stronger side than he had in previous third round FA Cup ties. He felt that the club needed a boost and he had to put out the strongest side he could to win the game. Therefore, there were starts for Ryan Fraser and Harry Wilson, along with Philip Billing in midfield. It would also be another chance for Dominic Solanke to try and get his first competitive goal for the club, and for once, he didn't disappoint.

As early as the first five minutes, Solanke made a great run and had a shot saved by Luton's keeper. Better luck befell Philip Billing on eight minutes when he volleyed home the opener and his first goal for the Cherries. It nearly became two-nil on 15 minutes when Solanke headed in from a corner, but Harry Wilson was adjudged by VAR to be offside and the goal was ruled out.

Things almost became a lot worse when, former Cherry player, Harry Cornick raced through to take on Mark Travers in the Bournemouth goal but had his shot saved. Billing had given the ball away to Cornick, and again found himself caught out when he fouled Matthew Pearson in the box. A penalty was awarded to Luton. It was pretty well right on half-time and the game hung in the balance. Luckily for Bournemouth, Alan Sheehan could only hit the penalty shot against the bar and Bournemouth survived to go in at the break 1-0 up.

The second half would be a much more productive 45 minutes for the Cherries. The match swung further in Bournemouth's favour just a minute after Callum Wilson replaced Junior Stanislas. Bournemouth's goal machine wasted no time in turning in a cross from Harry Wilson to make it 2-0 on 68 minutes.

Philip Billing then scored his second, and Bournemouth's third, just 10 minutes later. The game was won, but Dominic Solanke still kept plugging away and finally got his reward when he finished a close-range poacher's goal to make it 4-0. Bournemouth had safely progressed to the fourth round of the FA Cup for the first time in four seasons.

Moreover, Eddie Howe and the home crowd had reconnected and the players were cheered off the field with the fans knowing how important it was for the players to be confident ahead of their next Premier League game.

There was no early transfer window action for the Cherries, but Brad Smith had returned from his loan spell at Seattle Sounders to train with the Cherries. Kyle Taylor was also recalled from his loan at Forest Green Rovers. Eddie Howe then told the press that Mark Travers was too important at the moment to be released on loan. That was despite Asmir Begović also returning to the Cherries, having served out his loan spell at Qarabağ Agdam FK in Kazakhstan.

The FA Cup draw would put Bournemouth at home against 13-time winners Arsenal in the fourth round, but the league was the important priority. I expect most fans were like me in thinking that we'd rather see Bournemouth get safe in the league than go on a big cup run.

It was all about getting numbers back for the league matches and it was a question of how many would be available for the Watford game. Eddie Howe was going to leave journalists in suspense at his press conference as to which players might be returning for the game.

While which players would be fit was one thought on fans' minds, there was also a lot of gossip about whether Jordon Ibe or Nathan Aké would still be at the club at the end of January. Nathan Aké was reportedly likely to sign for Chelsea, as they had put a clause in his 2017 contract, when he signed for Bournemouth, giving them the first right to re-sign him for £40m. It was a shrewd business plan by Chelsea and it was likely that Eddie Howe could do nothing about matters, if Nathan Aké decided he want off.

I talked about the transfer speculation regarding Nathan Aké on *Cherry Chimes* on 10 January 2020. 'While Chelsea has its problems in shifting Andreas Christiansen to make room for Aké, we still don't know if Nathan would rather stay at Bournemouth with his team-mates, and fight on, in the relegation worrying season,' I explained.

I was quite clear about my thoughts on the matter. I didn't think Bournemouth should necessarily fear they would be relegated, just because they could lose their best defender. 'The task for Bournemouth is to find more central defenders that have the as good control and alertness as Aké. Even if Aké stays now, he is likely to be tempted away in the summer. He is good enough to be a Chelsea player and Bournemouth has benefited greatly from having him at the club. We can't stop him developing when he needs to try and force his way into the Netherlands' starting line-up,' I added.

While Nathan Aké's future remained unresolved, there was perhaps more of a possibility that Jordon Ibe would be leaving in January. The tabloids had decided to link the winger with Crystal Palace and Bournemouth fans were already aware that Brendan Rodgers at Leicester City had also shown some interest in Ibe, as a former Liverpool man who Rodgers had worked with before.

Bournemouth's scouting was perhaps not proving to be that amazing when it came to buying Liverpool players. There was a history of signings gone bad with Brad Smith and Dominic Solanke finding it hard to get going at the Cherries. But Jordon Ibe had been a record £15m signing when he had joined AFC Bournemouth and he hadn't lived up to the hype.

'The jury was always out on Ibe who has often tempted fans into thinking he could become a match-winner, but more often than not failed to live up to his suggested pedigree. Bournemouth might have had little choice but to buy players that had found it hard to make their way in the Premier League. Now they have found that strategy doesn't always pay off,' I wrote on *Cherry Chimes*.

Things just hadn't been going well for Bournemouth and that feeling continued when Chris Mepham announced on Friday 10 January that he had sustained a bad enough knee injury against Luton to need an operation, which was likely to keep him out for 12 weeks. That meant that the injured defenders now included Chris Mepham, Nathan Aké, Charlie Daniels, Adam Smith, Jack Stacey, and Lloyd Kelly.

The only recognisable defenders that were available to play for the Watford match were Simon Francis, Steve Cook, Brad Smith, Diego Rico and Jack Simpson. It was just as well that we still had senior statesman, Andrew Surman was fit and well, because at this rate he could be used as a makeshift defender.

Having had a real battering over the Christmas period, AFC Bournemouth decide that training needed a different angle in January. Therefore, Eddie Howe took the team to Steve Bendall's Gym in Parkstone to get them in a fighting mood ahead of the scraps they now had ahead of them. While the skills you have with your feet might be different in boxing bouts, compared to football, the mental feelings about stepping into the ring and walking onto the pitch were similar argued Eddie Howe.

The gloves were certainly on for Mark Travers who got his first Premier League start of the season against Watford. Unfortunately, Aaron Ramsdale had injured his hamstring in training. Bournemouth also saw the return of Nathan Aké from injury as well as Adam Smith. While the team prepared for the match with Watford, the club announced that Asmir Begović would be having a medical at AC Milan and would join them on loan.

Scoring goals was the immediate problem for the Cherries. They didn't manage much first half apart from a free kick from Harry Wilson. Then everything fell apart when Bournemouth tried to play out from the back, just before half-time. Simon Francis shifted the ball back to Travers who got the ball stuck under his foot, before making a clearance that went straight to Watford's Ismaïla Sarr. The ball was quickly crossed back into the box and Abdoulaye Doucouré had the goal at his mercy to give Watford the lead.

Eddie Howe soon saw the game go further away when Troy Deeney lashed in a second on 65 minutes. Even with a double midfield substitution of Lerma and Gosling, for Billing and Lewis Cook, Bournemouth couldn't get their passing going. It was left to substitute Roberto Pereyra to finish the Cherries off 0-3 much to the delight of the travelling Watford fans, who moved out of the relegation zone and put Bournemouth firmly in it, in 19th spot.

Working out how Bournemouth had slipped further into trouble was the week's work. There had been boos in the immediate aftermath of the defeat and Eddie Howe had said in an interview that he would have to consider his position.

I was not too keen on seeing Eddie Howe dwell too much on his role in the current problems. 'Eddie doesn't need to reflect on his position – get behind him,' I entitled the blog post after the Watford defeat. It was a simple analysis for me. 'Perhaps he has stayed too long and the play and players have become stale. But do I want Eddie to fall on his sword? No, absolutely not.'

The Cherries were struggling and they had handed one of their fellow strugglers three points. With just one goal in their last six league games, Bournemouth needed remedies. They had also let in seven goals in their last two games. You could say the wheels had fallen off, or perhaps disintegrated.

A couple of days after the Watford defeat I was contacted by the editor of *Buzz Sports*, the Bournemouth University magazine. Luke Donnelly wanted to ask me what most Bournemouth fans were talking about – Is Eddie Howe going to get Bournemouth out of this situation? I had to admit if the team couldn't beat Norwich in the next game it was looking very difficult to see how they could gain regain the points they would need with the tough fixtures to come. I was also asked about who might do a better job, and I struggled to see who. If Mauricio Pochettino came in, would he be ready for a relegation battle? He was certainly the only top-class manager that I felt could work well with the young players at Bournemouth, but I couldn't see him relishing a job that could land him in the Championship. It would be better for the club to stick with Eddie and see if he could turn things around than take a risk. We know what we are getting with Eddie and the team needed encouragement and tweaking, not a complete revolution in my mind.

It's funny how, as a fan, you can believe that the problems are mainly down to how you personally react to events. I often feel that I am responsible for the bad luck, and that if I expect the worst to happen, it will. It's like not changing your routine, having a superstition like not changing your club shirt until the club loses a game, or just feeling down about your team's prospects. We all get down when things are going wrong and, as a fan there is not much we can do about it apart from continue to show up, shout for our team and hope things turnaround.

Managers like Eddie Howe get paid the money to find the solutions and get results. It's a very difficult business when a bad run extends over five games. For

Bournemouth, it was one win in 11, and the last three teams Bournemouth had won points off were Manchester United, Chelsea and Arsenal. So how could the confidence have been shot against teams battling in mid-table?

In the pre-match press conference, Eddie Howe said they had reviewed everything about the preparation for the Watford game and looked to learn and see what they could do better for the Norwich City match. Eddie Howe was not getting drawn into the negative thoughts of others but was simply looking for ways to improve. Changing the results and performances was going to need a change of mood. Defensively the team had to do better and there had to be a shift in the team's attacking play.

Callum Wilson hadn't scored since September and Eddie Howe was adamant that he would score and get goals when the team itself improved.

On the injuries for the game, Eddie Howe confirmed that both Josh King and Jack Stacey were ruled out of playing Norwich City. It was a chance for Philip Billing, Diego Rico and Callum Wilson to come back into the starting eleven, and to see if they could turnaround Bournemouth's fortunes.

The away support for Bournemouth was over 1300 and the supporters were cheerful enough as the game got underway. The only thing that annoyed me was that Norwich made Bournemouth's players warm up in the half furthest away from our fans.

The match was fairly even for the first half-hour. Callum Wilson had had an early header saved, Billing blasted a shot over and Harry Wilson had come close to being played through, but had been flagged offside. Norwich had their chances too with a corner and Kenny McLean having a strong shot blocked, before Norwich's captain, Alexander Tettey, had a shot go wide.

The setback came for Bournemouth when Ramsdale made a good save before Ondrej Duda followed up and Steve Cook saved the shot with his hands and glanced the ball onto the post. It was a clear handball and it was a red card for Steve Cook. VAR confirmed it should be a penalty and Teemu Pukki put the ball into the roof of the net, down the middle. Bournemouth fell a goal down after 31 minutes.

There was a quick substitution for Bournemouth with Harry Wilson making way for Simon Francis to make up for the loss of Steve Cook. The rest of the half saw Norwich go closest to extending their lead with Todd Cantwell trying a volley, and Tettey shooting wildly from distance.

Emi Buendia was Norwich's player that seemed to be getting the better of Bournemouth. Then a chance finally fell to Callum Wilson, when Fraser crossed from the left. Unfortunately, Wilson slipped and from six-yards out he didn't connect. Bournemouth started to make a few mistakes with Fraser misdirecting a pass that almost let in Pukki. Ramsdale started to have to make a few impressive saves. The first was from Pukki who was fed in, one against one. Tettey then saw his shot saved low to his right, before Buendia beat most of the left side of Bournemouth's team, only to see Ramsdale save his shot.

The game might have turned when Godfrey was red carded on 78 minutes for fouling Callum Wilson. VAR agreed it was red. Paul Tierney even checked the monitor to confirm his decision. It gave Bournemouth a bit of momentum and at 10 against 10 again, Aké drove a header at goal that was tipped over by Tim Krul.

Ramsdale was still having to clear balls off the line at the other end as the game finished. Bournemouth just hadn't done enough. Norwich were just three points behind the Cherries now on 17 points and Bournemouth remained second bottom, while Watford had picked up another point, and so had Brighton and West Ham United, who were all moving away towards safety.

Eddie Howe didn't feel there had been a lot between Norwich City and Bournemouth, but just staying in the game wasn't what he wanted from the match. The players hadn't shown enough belief, even though they had done well with 10-men for most of the match.

Before we could blink and digest the result, the team had to prepare for Brighton & Hove Albion on a

Tuesday night. Fighting back and being consistent is what Eddie Howe wanted the energy to be focused on. Internally, Eddie didn't want anyone to be saying that the team was not good enough to stay up. It was them against us mentality now. Internally, Bournemouth's players knew outsiders would be writing them off. The players were hurting, but only a win could change that mood.

One bit of good news Eddie Howe mentioned in his pre-match press conference was that Lloyd Kelly was close to making a return, having played in a reserve game for 60 minutes. However, he might not be fit enough to play a Premier League match. Josh King and Jack Stacey were still out as well as Chris Mepham.

Bournemouth played Brighton under the floodlights at Dean Court. The evening games have a special atmosphere, and even though Brighton imposed themselves more in the first half-hour, the home crowd could find their voice when Harry Wilson slotted in the opening goal on 36 minutes. It was the first goal the Cherries had scored in some seven hours of play. It was Dominic Solanke who provided the assist, and he started to play some of his best football since arriving on the south coast. I can't say it hadn't been a long time coming.

The Cherries would enter half-time in a stronger position still, as an in-swinging corner from Diego Rico foxed Brighton's defence and Callum Wilson claims he got a touch before the ball went in off Pascal Groß on 41 minutes. Brighton had bossed the game with 65 per cent of possession, but they were 2-0 down. Lady luck had finally turned in Bournemouth's favour and the half-time chat would be a bit different from what it had been like in the past few weeks for Eddie Howe.

There was no worry that Brighton would get back into the game. Bournemouth kept pressing them high and causing them to panic at the back before Callum Wilson pretty much wrapped the game up by rounding Matthew Ryan to make it 3-0 on 74 minutes. It was all going well and the only question was whether Bournemouth could keep a clean sheet. Ramsdale had been magnificent and had kept Brighton at bay with some fantastic saves at key moments, but he couldn't stop a shot driven by Aaron Mooy, which went in off the right post on 81 minutes.

Aaron Ramsdale had been beaten, but he had had a good night. He was annoyed that he hadn't managed to keep a clean sheet and blasted Diego Rico for not doing more to stop the cross that came in for Aaron Mooy to get on the ball and make space for his goal. Still, Ramsdale could console himself with his award of player of the month for January.

It was a shame that there was no clean sheet but the win was such a relief. It was only the third home win of the season, and it took Bournemouth back above Watford on goal difference on 23 points from

24 games. Bournemouth would probably need six more wins to be sure of safety before the end of the season. It was going to be a struggle to achieve that but it was possible. West Ham was a point ahead, with Aston Villa and Brighton on 25 points.

Harry Wilson was proving to be a fantastic loan signing as he topped the Cherries' goal chart with seven league goals. Without him, it would be hard to see where Bournemouth would be, and that is why I felt the loss of David Brooks was not being felt as much as many people wanted to make out. It was in other areas where Bournemouth struggled, not the right-wing.

Eddie Howe felt that the team hadn't yet performed to its true abilities and was still short of a complete performance, but the players had hopefully turned a corner. He thought it was like watching a different team once the first goal had gone in as all the confidence came flooding back. It hadn't been a technical issue that had been stopping Bournemouth from winning any of their previous six league games, it was a confidence issue, he concluded.

Bournemouth's win would not have been possible without the saves of Aaron Ramsdale. He had become the solid figure who was consistently outperforming everyone else. Playing with a smile on his face, he almost relished the pressure to perform in the relegation scrap. I suggested that Bournemouth wrap him up in cotton wool.

One player Bournemouth would not have to be thinking about much longer was Jermain Defoe. He had been on loan up at Rangers. He decided he would not only carry on playing for them up to the summer but would also sign a pre-contract to sign for the Scottish club permanently in the summer.

With the January transfer window getting ready to close, Bournemouth hadn't signed any new players but no one had left. None of the rumours seemed that credible. If anything, the team needed a striker, so it seemed puzzling that Jermain Defoe was allowed to stay up at Rangers. But there surely had to be some reason why Eddie Howe didn't see Defoe as a player that could offer Bournemouth anything more.

Immediate thoughts turned to the FA Cup fourth round. Bournemouth would have to wait until Monday 27 January before taking on Arsenal under the lights at Dean Court.

Philip Billing felt his back in the warm-up and was withdrawn from the squad, while Lloyd Kelly felt a slight discomfort on his ankle again and missed out on the game. The night didn't get any better with Arsenal going ahead on six minutes when Bukayo Saka slashed the ball into the net past Travers. If Arsenal had been moving fluently and getting shots on target, Bournemouth had been chasing shadows. A second goal on 26 minutes from Eddie Nketiah pretty much decided the tie. Bournemouth hoped to avoid embarrassment. There was a bit of a rally though after half-time. It was a good job as the Cherries had only had 37 per cent of possession in the first half and had managed just three shots with one on target. While Jack Simpson had a good chance to head in from a corner, chances were still hard to come by, until substitute Sam Surridge scored his first goal for Bournemouth in the 90+4 minute to make it 1-2. Even then, there was a last-minute chance for Lewis Cook to take the game to a replay when he blasted his shot over.

The opening period of the Arsenal game was tough for Bournemouth. They just didn't compete well enough. The game got away from the players quickly, but they did much better in the second half. Eddie Howe pointed to a lack of zip and aggression in the first half. But the way the team finished was a vast improvement and the team had created six chances since the Brighton match.

Sam Surridge's first goal for the club was huge for him. It didn't make much of a difference to the result, but it would have convinced him that he belongs at this level. Surridge wasn't given many minutes to impress by coming on until the 89th minute, but he certainly got noticed with his well-taken finish.

Going out of the FA Cup at the fourth round was disappointing, but mainly for the knowledge that we all knew that the next game would have been against Portsmouth if Bournemouth had progressed. The draw for the next round had been made before the match with Arsenal. Arsenal would go on to win the cup, beating Chelsea in the final in an empty Wembley Stadium.

Now Bournemouth had nothing else to concentrate but their Premier League survival. Eddie Howe made it fairly clear that it was unlikely Bournemouth would be bringing anyone in before the close of the January window. There was a chance that Jack Simpson could be taken on loan by a Championship side, as Stoke City, Derby County and Middlesbrough had shown interest. But Howe was adamant that Simpson was going nowhere. I felt Simpson had been the best Bournemouth player against Arsenal and couldn't have done much more himself in the game.

As we came up to the Transfer Deadline window, there was some trepidation for AFC Bournemouth fans. Manchester United put a surprise bid in for Josh King to bolster their striking options. Eddie Howe said the decision would be out of his hands and would rest with the Chairman and club owner if they wanted to sell. The bid was knocked back and yet Manchester United still thought they might try a loan deal to the end of the season. Luckily, despite King's affinity with the Manchester club from his youth career, there was to be no further move for him this window.

To lose such an experienced striker on the last day of the transfer window would have been a nightmare for Eddie Howe to try and get a replacement. While

Josh was injured, it was hoped that he would be back in action soon and fans were just pleased that he would still be wearing a Bournemouth shirt when that happened.

Bournemouth did let Matt Butcher go out on loan to St Johnstone to the end of the season, but none of the regular first-team starters were sold. It was therefore seen as a good window for the Cherries. They had held on to Callum Wilson, Ryan Fraser and Nathan Aké.

# Chapter 8.
# February – In the mire

With the January Transfer Window now shut, all minds could now focus on the crunch relegation game against Aston Villa. While Aston Villa sat outside the bottom three, Bournemouth found themselves still deep in trouble in 18th place. A win would lift Bournemouth out of the relegation zone and would complete a double win against Villa if they could achieve it.

1 February was greeted with plenty of sunshine at Dean Court for the afternoon game. Eddie Howe decided just to play Callum Wilson as the main striker, with Ryan Fraser and Harry Wilson on either side. The midfield was packed with Jefferson Lerma, Dan Gosling and Philip Billing, while there was no place for Steve Cook in the back four, which included a recovered Diego Rico and captain Simon Francis.

The game began well with Bournemouth almost getting the perfect early start. Harry Wilson saw his half-hit shot into the ground, nearly headed in by Adam Smith, but the defender just put his header wide of Pepe Reina's post. The Cherries attacked with purpose and kicked long with Aaron Ramsdale to put the ball in Villa's half as much as they could. Dan Gosling had the next big chance to score when Harry Wilson pulled a ball back for him from the byline, but the birthday boy kept his head up and his shot spooned over the bar, from just outside the six-yard box. It was strange to see the Cherries kicking towards the North stand in the first half, but they had started with great momentum. The pressure paid off when Simon Francis lobbed a deep ball to the far post, where Gosling headed back across the six-yard box for Philip Billing to run on and score his first Premier League goal for AFC Bournemouth on 37 minutes.

The home crowd was enjoying the moment and it felt like this would be the Cherries' day. It was just as well the Cherries had scored, as Watford and West Ham were also winning and would all be looking to move away from the bottom of the table. The smiles grew even wider at Dean Court when on 44 minutes. Ryan Fraser's shot was spilled by Pepe Reina and Nathan Aké was alert enough to react quickest to make it 2-0.

With the game seemingly going Bournemouth's way, it was great to have a half-time when the team had done well. They had pressed high on Villa and had kept the play in the Villa half apart from a few raids from the talented Jack Grealish. The second half would be a tighter affair.

Jefferson Lerma had already been booked for a foul on Grealish, during an Aston Villa breakaway in the first half. There had been a few niggly matters that referee Anthony Taylor had let go, but when Lerma stood his ground and Grealish tried to run past him, knocking the Columbian to the floor, Taylor viewed it as deliberate obstruction, and handed Lerma a second yellow card and consequently a red card on 51 minutes. Bournemouth now had to play out forty-minutes of the match with just 10-men.

Usually, Eddie Howe would consider making a substitute in such a position, but he just lined up Callum Wilson in front of two banks of four and carried on. The team responded well until Francis' block on a shot from Davis bounced up high in Bournemouth's box. The Tanzanian Samatta won the race to the ball ahead of Ramsdale and headed in a goal for Villa with 20 minutes to go.

It was Bournemouth that would now be under pressure. Grealish had already gone close with a shot that went through Ramsdale's legs and just missed going in at the far post. Now Ramsdale was having to be extra alert, as he started to fall on a few loose balls that peppered Bournemouth's box. The clean sheet had gone, but the players were doing all they could to keep Villa out and they held on for a great 2-1 win. The result was greeted with such enjoyment that the players didn't seem to want to leave the pitch. They came back out to have a group huddle with all the staff and were given a rapturous cheer from the home crowd that had stayed to thank them for their efforts. We could go home happy in the knowledge that the Cherries had moved up to 16$^{th}$ in the table, with 26 points from their 25 games. They had jumped ahead of West Ham United and Aston Villa with the three points.

The match will be remembered as much for the post-match group huddle on the pitch, which we subsequently found out was led by Steve Fletcher. The players needed to soak up some of the good feelings following the win and Steve Fletcher was not going to let the staff and players forget how good it was to get the win and to keep the momentum building. The group huddle was therefore the starting point for my week's review on *Cherry Chimes*.

'It was a heart-warming scene at the end of the match against Aston Villa. The players looked genuinely relieved by the result and delighted in the way that they had played. It was all the more important for a win because they had done it with 10-men in the second half and had finally managed to escape the bottom three.'

I still felt there was a lot of work to be done, but it was a start. 'The results are starting to come now and it is pleasing to think Bournemouth might have turned the corner, but the team has to go and beat teams that are above them in the table now if they are to pull away from those teams around them. The challenges are still there, and the ring of friendship at the end of the Aston Villa match will hopefully push the players on to more delightful scenes at the end of the next few games,' I added.

The next talking point was to work out how this sudden upturn in form had happened. My theory was that it had helped the team massively to get the ball forward quickly – call it long ball, call it missing out the midfield, or just Ramsdale starting moves with his booming goal kick – Bournemouth were no longer getting pressed in front of their own goal.

'There was a different game plan for Aston Villa that worked extremely well in the first half-hour. Instead of taking their time to get the ball forward, Bournemouth went long and drilled long passes and goal kicks up into the Villa half, and won the knockdowns to get themselves on the front foot.

'The quick start to the game by Bournemouth was certainly helped by the way the players looked to win the ball back quickly and press when Villa did get possession. It was all fast playing and it didn't give Villa a chance to slow things down and settle. I am not sure why the game is sometimes harder to do the same things from one day to the next, but for once Bournemouth carried out their game plan and it was effective,' I continued.

There was another element to the change in the way the team was operating as well. I didn't disguise the fact that it had been a difficult past few months, but lessons had surely been learned.

'It has been hard to watch the Cherries at times this season. At times you just wanted to turn the radio off rather than listen to more criticism about just how poor the Cherries had been playing. But with the team suddenly stringing a couple of wins together and the table looking a bit easier to look at, Bournemouth's players have been enjoying their football again. That is what has been missing in my opinion more than anything else. The players were feeling sorry for themselves. Now they are hungry to get results and to punish other teams – it has made the world of difference,' I commented.

I felt all the players had contributed to the win and while I gave man if the match to Adam Smith, in the main for his goal-line clearance in the second half, it was Simon Francis that was getting many of the plaudits. He had kept his place ahead of Steve Cook and had given everything in the game. I didn't fail to remind supporters of how well Francis had played and said that he was far from finished at AFC Bournemouth.

'Simon Francis has had his fair share of knockers this season. He must be approaching the end of his Premier League career, but he's not going without trying to recapture some of his old form. Against Aston Villa, it was a surprise to see him start ahead of

Steve Cook, but during the game, he showed why he was worth the starting place.

'Francis was also instrumental in setting up Bournemouth's first goal with the cross to Dan Gosling. I think we have forgotten what a good crosser of the ball he has been in his career and he did well to pick Gosling out. But it was the defensive game of Francis that was particularly strong against Villa. Francis was determined to win his challenges and I thought he was an inspiration to the rest of the team on the day,' I added.

Fans couldn't ignore the fact that Jefferson Lerma had been sent off. Anthony Taylor had waved his cards and for the second card Lerma received for allegedly blocking Jack Grealish, he was off. Eddie Howe seemed dumbfounded by the decision. He stated that Lerma had nowhere to go and I also thought Grealish had just lunged at Lerma, knocking him off his feet.

I didn't mince my words on the blog. 'The first was a mistimed tackle and it warranted a yellow card. What was getting our backs up though was that Anthony Taylor wasn't being consistent with his yellow cards.

'There was no intent from Lerma to block off Grealish, he was simply standing in front of Villa's attacker and was taken by surprise when Grealish decided he would try to run at Bournemouth's number eight. The referee clearly saw something very different, but it was annoying that VAR could not be used to correct a misjudgement. It easily could have cost Bournemouth the game and the referee seemed to have it in for Lerma with the way he didn't even listen to Simon Francis' pleas to be consistent with the fouls that other players had been making and getting away with,' I added.

For all Bournemouth's midfield problems with Lerma, who seemed to be a target now for referees, there was good cause to be very happy with the form of Philip Billing. It was great to see his first Premier League goal for the Cherries, and so quickly after he got his first goal in the FA Cup for the club.

'Philip Billing has started this year well with goals against Luton Town and now Aston Villa. The goal against Villa was pleasing, as it was a good team goal with Francis recovering Fraser's free kick and putting in a deep cross for Gosling to knockdown. Billing came from the blindside and passed the ball into the net with some precision. He didn't over hit it and knew he'd scored the instant he connected with the ball,' I commented.

Nathan Aké was the other unlikely goalscorer against Aston Villa. His anticipation was essential in following up Ryan Fraser's drive that Pepe Reina could only parry out. Aké had the desire to get there first and while the suspense for the decision from VAR to see if he was offside was a little prolonged, it was jubilation when the goal stood.

Bournemouth would be without Jefferson Lerma for their next match against Sheffield United, but I didn't feel that it would be such a big miss, as he had been at other times when the Cherries were struggling more.

Philip Billing and Dan Gosling had been great against Villa and I expected them to carry that on at Bramall Lane. But there was competition in midfield.

'Lewis Cook and Andrew Surman are the other options for Howe, but the side has been winning of late. Gosling and Billing have been big players in recent games and are getting forward well. It's not the time to make too many changes and Eddie Howe knows he has a stable midfield if he picks Billing and Gosling,' I concluded.

The one position that we knew would be safe was in goal. Aaron Ramsdale was having a cracking season and he would be bubbling up inside about a trip back to Bramall Lane, as I explained on the blog.

'Going back to Bramall Lane will be inspirational for him I hope, and I expect there is nowhere he would rather get his fifth clean sheet of the season.

'I was a bit shocked that Aaron blamed himself for the goal that Aston Villa scored against Bournemouth in the last game. He might have been a bit slower than he wanted in going to make the punch, but I am not sure he was ever going to be favourite to get there first. He can put that behind him now though, and look to try and get his fifth clean sheet as a ground that will mean a lot to him,' I felt.

I found myself almost in as much demand as Aaron Ramsdale when I got a phone call at work to see if I could appear on *TalkSport 2* for a few minutes one February afternoon. The radio station was doing a relegation special and asking bloggers from the bottom six clubs if they would give an update on how things were at their respective clubs before the run-in started in earnest. I was only asked a couple of questions, starting with whether I had sensed a change in things at Bournemouth with the last two wins. Indeed, it had been a much better feeling in supporters' bellies now that the club had risen out of the drop zone, and had a couple of good home wins under its belt. But I knew the Cherries were not out of the woods yet, and the away from would have to improve.

What had changed was the way the club had united both fans and players. We were in this together and the after-match huddle at Dean Court, following the win over Aston Villa, gave me a real sense that the players were ready for the fight ahead.

The team was also getting the ball forward much quicker and playing their football in the opposition's half. It had relieved the pressure for the moment, and seeing them do the right things was just a relief after the disappointing shows during December and January.

I was then asked about whether the club had been right to stick with Eddie Howe? It was an easy answer to say yes because Eddie had started to get results again. More than that, I explained that Eddie knew how to win games in the Premier League and that had never left him. A lot had been said about the injuries contributing to the poor results, but Eddie Howe was not the main reason why the team had been on such a bad run. We all knew he worked harder than ever when the team was not winning, but we were just as relieved as him to see the team improve and start picking up points again. A happy Eddie Howe is what we want to see, and that comes with winning games.

Eddie was less pleased with hearing about a so-called Bournemouth fan that had been in front of the magistrates for racist remarks at the game back in November against Tottenham Hotspur. The courts gave the young 17-year-old a three-year ban, but that was quickly extended to a life ban by AFC Bournemouth. It was a clear message to send out to fans that racism would not be tolerated at Dean Court.

As the time drew closer to the match with Sheffield United, I had a couple of conversations with Sheffield United fans on Rival Lines. The first was *Blades Podcast* that stressed that the signing of Lys Mousset, the former Bournemouth striker, had been 'Amazing!' While a lot of rubbish had been said about

Lys as their worst signing of the season, Lys had shown that he was Premier League quality. They just needed him to get fitter and play for 90 minutes rather than 60 minutes.

I couldn't disagree. What Mousset had done since he arrived at Sheffield United had been remarkable, when compared with his misfiring career at AFC Bournemouth. The only worry I had was that he would be more fired up than ever to score against the Cherries, when the two sides would meet on 9 February 2020.

The press conference that Eddie Howe gave for Sheffield United was keenly viewed with attention turning to the preparedness of Josh King. It was coincidental that the Premier League clubs were talking about mental health this week when Eddie was asked is Josh King's head in the right place having missed out on a move to Manchester United? Of course, it had been disappointing for Josh, but it was great news for AFC Bournemouth, and Josh was now training with the team and expected to be available for selection again. Eddie had no doubts that King was fully committed to the cause and that he wanted to help Bournemouth out of the trouble they have been in.

The news on David Brooks was also positive in that the Welsh winger had been training on grass again for the first time since his second operation. He was still probably two-three weeks off being a selection choice, but with no minor pain of uncomfortableness in his ankle, it was hoped he'd be back soon.

Jack Stacey was also back training, so the competition was, at last, starting to return to the squad with Stanislas and Steve Cook also pushing for starts.

One player who wouldn't make the team, because he was an old returning Cherry was Brett Pitman. Portsmouth hadn't needed his services, so he had asked to train with Bournemouth's U21s and U18s back at Dean Court just to keep fit.

As the Sunday morning of the Sheffield United match arrived for Bournemouth fans, they were greeted with storm Ciara which blew in 80-90mph winds and battered the UK. While Manchester City's game against West Ham United was called off, Bournemouth's game was allowed to go ahead at Bramall Lane.

Bournemouth brought in Andrew Surman to the starting line-up instead of Jefferson Lerma and Jack Stacey and Josh King made it to the subs bench. The game started as well as we could have hoped with Bournemouth putting pressure on the Sheffield United goal, and Ryan Fraser's early cross being almost converted by Harry Wilson. The blocked shot came out to Callum Wilson, and he fired the Cherries ahead on 13 minutes. At that point, it was looking great for a possible three points and a five-point gap over the bottom three. But Sheffield United had their reasons for looking to win the game. A win for them would take them into fifth place.

Sure enough, United would do all they could to apply pressure on Bournemouth's goal. As we entered added time at the end of the first half, Bournemouth failed to clear a corner with Aaron Ramsdale missing his punch clear. The ball was crossed again into the box, and Billy Sharp stuck a foot out to score and make it 1-1 at half-time.

Eddie Howe looked reluctant to change anything in the second half despite coming under more attacks from the Blades. Bournemouth did fashion a great chance for Ryan Fraser, that Callum Wilson assisted with, but Henderson in the Sheffield United goal made a great save, to his left, to keep the scores tied. Nathan Aké also flashed a shot wide from a corner, but the game looked destined for a draw as we entered the last 10 minutes.

We'd not have been happy with a point, but it would have been better than nothing. Just as Junior Stanislas was brought on for the last six minutes, Sheffield tried another attack up the left, and Lys Mousset played a low cross to John Lundstram, who scored and ensured all three points would be going to United. It was a punishing defeat and the Bournemouth players knew they had thrown the game away.

What fans didn't know at the time is that referee

Jonathan Moss was also giving verbal stick to the players during the match. Dan Gosling reported that the referee had shown no respect for the Bournemouth players with his comments about how they were having a nightmare and that they would be stuck in the bottom three. At first AFC Bournemouth looked at having the claims investigated, but they decided that the Premier League would never act against a referee, so let the matter drop.

One matter that the national press didn't seem to want to drop was Josh King's failed move to Manchester United. *The Athletic* was back on the saga on 17 February when it claimed that Ed Woodward, Chief Executive at Manchester United had spoken to Neill Blake personally about the King transfer. Having submitted a bid of £25m for the Norwegian striker, Woodward was said to have given Bournemouth an ultimatum of just 15 minutes to decide if they wanted to do the deal or not.

It turned out that Manchester United did a loan deal instead for Odion Ighalo the former Watford striker from Shanghai Greenland Shenhua of the Chinese Super League. Bournemouth were not offered a loan deal and let the deadline pass, without believing that Woodward was really serious about his short deadline.

Whether Manchester United really wanted Josh King or not the transfer would have been a massive decision for Neill Blake as it came out of the blue. It was no surprise that no decision was made to adhere to Woodward's deadline. After all, Bournemouth were in a relegation battle, and losing one of their best players was never going to be an easy decision, even if the valuation was deemed adequate for the player. There certainly wouldn't be any time for Bournemouth to get a replacement in, and so it was the player that would have to reflect on what might have been, while Bournemouth kept their £25m striker for the run-in.

While storm Dennis had done its worst in the week, the remnants of the strong winds still hung around Turf Moor for Bournemouth's journey up north. Bournemouth had to play without Jefferson Lerma who had a back injury and Nathan Aké who had been concussed in training in the week. It meant that Jack Stacey would come back into the team in place of Diego Rico, while Josh King and Steve Cook also won starts.

The wind was with Bournemouth in the first half and the chances started to come quickly with Callum Wilson missing the first opportunity, as Nick Pope stuck out a saving foot. Matěj Vydra should have scored at the other end as well, in the first quarter of an hour, but Ramsdale made a great save to his left. Bournemouth started to make a few mistakes with Francis finding Jay Rodriguez a bit too quick for him, but the team rode their luck.

The luck might have gone Bournemouth's way

when a corner was flicked on by Billing and King got ahead of Callum Wilson to score, or so we thought. But VAR decided that Billing had knocked the ball on with his arm and the goal was struck off.

A backward header by Francis let Vydra in for a second time, but again Ramsdale showed that he is the best keeper in such situations, as he made another improbable save. At 0-0 at half-time, the game was still in the balance, but the wind would be with the Clarets in the second half.

It proved a different game second half with Vydra breaking away to get Burnley ahead on 53 minutes. Simon Francis had slid in trying to stop the forward but had merely sold himself short and opened up the goal for Vydra to slam the ball past Ramsdale.

That was bad enough, but the game would quickly turn even more. Adam Smith tried to clear a ball into Bournemouth's box and get the Cherries going forward. The ball was taken out of defence and Callum Wilson sped away before passing the ball to Harry Wilson, who snuck the ball past Pope and into the net. It was going to be all square, but then VAR took over. The goal would be disallowed as Adam Smith was judged to have handled the ball when stopping a cross in his own box, earlier in the move. Worse still, the Cherries would have to face a penalty and Jay Rodriguez made it 2-0 from the penalty spot on 61 minutes.

Nothing was going for Bournemouth and Stockley

Park might as well have been a swear word to away fans at Turf Moor. While the Cherries still threw men forward and brought on Stanislas, Fraser and Solanke, in an attempt to try and get on the scoreboard, a mistake by Billing on half-way led to another Burnley break. This time McNeil raced clear and picked out the top corner of Bournemouth's goal to make it 3-0 on 84 minutes. It was game over and Bournemouth had to reflect on the first half that had promised so much. The VAR decisions had gone the other way and a 3-0 defeat sounded very hard on the Cherries who had dominated the first 45 minutes. Luckily Brighton had only picked up a point at Sheffield United and Southampton had beaten Aston Villa to help the Cherries stay in 16th place, but something would be needed again to pick the players up before the visit of fourth-placed Chelsea.

While some of the build-up for the Chelsea game was dominated with talk in the local press about Harry Wilson's loan spell under Frank Lampard, at Derby County, there was no room for Harry Wilson in the starting line-up against Chelsea. Instead, Eddie Howe brought Ryan Fraser back into the team and he added Philip Billing, Lewis Cook and Steve Cook, as captain, to the starting line-up. Eddie dropped Simon Francis, Harry Wilson, Dan Gosling and Andrew Surman. The surprise choice was to play Lewis Cook in central midfield.

There was a good deal of apprehension before the

game among Bournemouth fans. Chelsea's midweek defeat in the Champions League against Bayern Munich gave our fans reason to believe their side could make it difficult for Chelsea, who would be on their third game in eight days. So, it turned out, with Bournemouth having chances in the first 10 minutes to open the scoring. Philip Billing was getting forward well and put one chance from a Jack Stacey cross right at Willy Caballero in the Chelsea goal. He then beat Fikayo Tomori to a ball from a throw-in and rattled the side netting, as Bournemouth pushed forward.

Chelsea tested Ramsdale as well with a shot from Mason Mount that bounced in front of the Bournemouth keeper, but Ramsdale managed to parry it away. Bournemouth had been less lucky on 33 minutes when Chelsea took charge with a cross from James that caught the Bournemouth defence out. While Ramsdale saved Olivier Giroud's well-directed header onto the bar and post, Marcos Alonso was on hand at the far post to volley in past Jack Stacey.

A goal down at half-time, Eddie Howe had one of his most effective half-time team talks of the season. Bournemouth came out for the second half with renewed vigour. But Chelsea should have been 0-2 up when Giroud missed a chance straight away from about six yards out.

Giroud was left feeling even worse when

Bournemouth took advantage of a corner to see Jefferson Lerma head the Cherries back into the game with a bullet header, and his first goal of the season on 54 minutes. Bournemouth stepped up the pressure with the crowd raging for more. They didn't have to wait long. Bournemouth's players responded with a lightning move down the right side. Jack Stacey and Philip Billing played a great passing move that led to Stacey crossing at first for Callum Wilson, and when he didn't connect, Josh King arrived perfectly at the far post to tap in for Bournemouth's second goal on 57 minutes.

The home crowd was buzzing. Bournemouth had scored two goals in three minutes. A vital three points were back on the table and the gap to the bottom three looked like it would be extended. The problem was the Cherries had to hang on for more than half an hour.

At first, it looked like Bournemouth might even extend the lead further. A headed knockdown from Nathan Aké provided Callum Wilson with an opportunity to spin and fire a low shot at Caballero, but the keeper saw the shot bounce off his frame to safety.

Bournemouth started to play deeper and deeper as the pressure from Chelsea for an equaliser came on. Junior Stanislas replaced Josh King on 68 minutes and Dan Gosling then came on for Lewis Cook on 81 minutes. With the last 10 minutes, Eddie Howe looked to hold out. Chelsea still had Bournemouth pinned back, and their luck came off when Mason Mount saw Ramsdale save his well-hit shot diving to his right, only for Marcos Alonso to grab his and Chelsea's second goal by heading in on 85 minutes.

The win had been snatched away from Bournemouth and there was nothing they had left to come back again. Yet again Bournemouth were made to feel that they had lost points which had almost been in their grasp. A point was something to take from the game, and it was just good to know that Bournemouth had played well against a top-four side.

Eddie Howe was calm in his response saying that it had been a great game and that it had been very entertaining with both teams playing well. But the frustration was there, as he knew it so easily could have been three points instead of one.

Later that evening though Bournemouth fans became aware that not only West Ham had picked up an important three points, Watford had won at home against the previously unbeaten Liverpool. The other results saw Bournemouth ending February third from bottom in the league on goal difference with only Aston Villa and Norwich City below them and Aston Villa had a game in hand.

# THE DISRUPTED SEASON (2019-20)

# Chapter 9. March – Coronavirus

The first week of March was packed with some off the pitch stories for Dean Court starting with Jordon Ibe, who found himself fined £7500 and banned from driving for 16 months after he had crashed his Bentley in London into a coffee shop last year.

If Ibe was feeling like he was short in the pocket he was soon joined by goalkeeping coach Neil Moss who was fined £1150 by the FA for his language and behaviour on the touchline, during the Bournemouth defeat to Burnley a few weeks earlier.

Keeping clean and washing hands of everything was the main talking point for everyone, as the Covid-19 virus was in full contagious mode, with the Premier League deciding that handshakes should no longer be performed before the start of games.

I was pleased to see that *Cherry Chimes* was not being avoided by *This is Anfield*, a Liverpool blog that wanted the inside fan thoughts ahead of Bournemouth's next game with Liverpool. Liverpool had just lost in their unbeaten record in the Premier League to Watford which had pushed Bournemouth down into the bottom three. Having also gone out of the FA Cup to Chelsea, Liverpool were in a bit of a mini-crisis, especially as they had lost their first leg of their Champions League tie, as well to Atletico Madrid. How lucky for them then I thought that their next game was against AF C Bournemouth.

*This is Anfield* asked me whether there was much optimism about the rest of our season? Here are my replies.

TIA: Bournemouth are 18th in the Premier League - what has gone wrong this season?

CC: Rather a lot has gone wrong, to be honest. The injuries have been long ones and they have kept key players out for important games. Charlie Daniels won't be back this season and it could be touch and go whether Arnaut Danjuma and Chris Mepham make it back, while we are still waiting for David Brooks to return, after two operations this season. But other players have missed several games like Callum Wilson, Josh King, Nathan Aké – the list goes on! I think it was a mistake to sell Lys Mousset to Sheffield United as well, as it left us with just three recognised strikers and Dominic Solanke hasn't exactly hit any form.

Add to all this, the team's inability to score more than about a goal a game, and a porous defence, and you can quickly see why Bournemouth are at the wrong end of the table.

TIA: Do you think the Cherries will beat the drop?

CC: When Bournemouth lost to Watford and then Norwich City in January, I didn't see the team have the fight to beat the drop. Those were games that could have built a gap between Bournemouth and the bottom three, but the team surrendered the points in games that could have given Bournemouth a lift. Now we have players coming back, but we have to play the top sides in the league. It isn't going to be easy. I did feel like the confidence returned against Chelsea in our last match, and at home, we seem back to our best. It is away from home where the worry is. We haven't picked up a point away in 2020 and that's not good enough.

There might be three worse teams, but it's hard to see Bournemouth not being involved in the drama on the last day of the season. I am pleased the club has stuck with Eddie Howe, as he deserves the loyalty after what he has done for the club. But this is his hardest challenge he has had to keep us up, and I just feel he can do it. It could be bad news in that case for Norwich City, Aston Villa and possibly Brighton & Hove Albion (although West Ham is capable of imploding as well). I think Watford will be fine. You have to have almost a nasty streak now to want to stay up, and I just hope Bournemouth play hard enough to get the points they need.

TIA: Which players have stood out most this season?

CC: Aaron Ramsdale in goal. He has been outstanding. He has such a great connection with the fans and it's been a real pleasure to see him play so well. He has been keeping the team in games and he enjoys his football so much. I can't see anyone else picking up any of the awards at the end of the season. Aaron deserves them all.

He has been involved in relegation battles for the last three seasons at Chesterfield and AFC Wimbledon, where he was on loan, and now at AFC Bournemouth, his parent club. He kept his previous teams up and we hope he is a good omen to keep the Cherries up.

TIA: How has Harry Wilson fared on loan from Liverpool?

CC: Harry has been one of the players that have performed well. He is a superb free kick specialist and he has no fear of taking on a shot anywhere in and around the box. He will be a great addition to your squad if Jurgen Klopp lets him come onto Liverpool's subs bench next season. He may have a bit to learn in his defensive duties, but he has been fully committed to AFC Bournemouth at the moment. We couldn't have expected anything better than what he has provided with seven goals.

TIA: How highly do you rate this Reds side among the best of the Premier League era?

CC: This is a phenomenal Liverpool team. I don't see many weaknesses and even the players that Klopp has on the bench can change a game. It's the understanding between Mané, Salah and Firmino that is great to watch. Trent-Alexander Arnold and Andrew Robinson are probably up there with the best wing-backs ever to have played in the league, while nobody gets past Virgil van Dyke. There may be individual players in the past that you could say we're as good or better than some members of the team, but I don't like Man Utd or Man City, Chelsea, while Arsenal won it so long ago that I'm happy to say Liverpool are the best to watch! It's great to see someone else win the title for a change, and Liverpool has a great history and a superb manager, so I think any neutral will be pleased for Liverpool fans.

TIA: What do you think is the key to their success?

CC: Jurgen Klopp is infections, his recruitment has been spot-on and the players wanted to do it for the fans. The players know it's been a long time in coming and to get so close last season just spurred them on to a superlative season. I do think Man City have fallen a long way from the standards they have set in the past, but that isn't Liverpool's fault. Liverpool should win it at a canter. They know they are currently the best. The next challenge for them will be to stay there. Without that desire of not having won the title, it will be interesting to see if the players have the same appetite to become serial winners. I think they have that, but everyone will be gunning to take Liverpool down now.

TIA: Who do you fear most for Liverpool on Saturday?

CC: Playing at Anfield is the worst problem. I hope your crowd has an off day and lose their voices for a bit. The Anfield roar gives you a goal head start. After that, you can almost take your pick on who is going to score against us. Last time it was the ex-Southampton player Alex Oxlade-Chamberlain – it's always an annoying prospect when an ex-Southampton player is on the pitch. The player who I think has been best for you though is Mané, perhaps he can be rested ahead of the Champions League match? Actually, can you have a word with Klopp to play your U21 side? I know they'd still be good enough to give us a very good game and might even be favourites to win, so why risk playing your best players with such an important European night to come?

TIA: Where will the key battles take place?

CC: It will probably be a fight between Ramsdale's gloves and rather a lot of shots from those in red shirts. Seriously though, our central defenders have to stand up and watch the movement and runs off your front players, while our full-backs have to try and stop crosses from your wing-backs. I think our supply route to goal has been shown *on Match of the Day* by Jermaine Jenas. He saw how good Jack Stacey is down the right side. If Jack can make Andrew Robinson think about having to defend a little more than normal then we'll be in the game.

If we can then stay in the game and frustrate Liverpool, you never know what could happen. Bournemouth are currently the top team from scoring at set-pieces after all. We need Josh King, Ryan Fraser and Callum Wilson to all have their shooting boots on and Ramsdale to show why he will soon be England's number one if we are to win.

TIA: Finally, hit us with your prediction...

CC: The head says it should be a comfortable 3-0 or 4-0 win for Liverpool. But football doesn't always go as expected, so I'm happy to stick my neck out and say Liverpool will dominate and have possession stats of 75 per cent or more, and yet find themselves tripped up by a single goal from a corner, headed in by Philip Billing, who never scores. But this time he might use his face, back, or knee (not his shoulder!) to good effect to give us the lead.

And while Liverpool will hit the post, the bar and see Ramsdale pummelled with shots, perhaps even score the old goal or two and they could have them all ruled out by VAR. AFC Bournemouth could then feel like the league has given them some luck back for the horrors that we have seen in the last few months go against us, and let us have a totally undeserved but gratefully received 0-1 away win! Now that would be a good away day for our fans.

With the Liverpool match analysis done for a fellow blogger, I had the opportunity to go and have a night out and my wife who had kindly bought tickets as a Christmas gift to an Audience with Harry Redknapp in Crawley, which we went along to in the first week of March. Harry was on top form telling jokes and stories about his career and managerial successes. He knew just about everyone in football and could name drop in every sentence. It was good to be in his company and to hear some more tales about AFC Bournemouth in a positive light. It was just the cheer up I needed before Bournemouth looked to take on the team who already had the title of World Club Champions.

The team news for the Liverpool match immediately knocked Bournemouth fans on the back foot. Josh King had not made the squad because of a hamstring strain. We already knew that Harry Wilson could not play against his parent club, so Junior Stanislas was brought in to replace Josh King on the left-wing. Liverpool played their top strikers and it was clear it would be a difficult afternoon, but to our surprise, a great move by Callum Wilson and Philip Billing put Jefferson Lerma in down the right side. Lerma's low cross to Callum Wilson saw Bournemouth take the lead on nine minutes. There was a VAR check on a barge by Callum Wilson in the build-up on Gomez, but the goal was allowed to stand.

The attacks came fast and Bournemouth could have gone 0-2 up, had Nathan Aké's header dipped below the bar.

The next moment, Bournemouth found themselves in trouble with Steve Cook overstretching to stop Firmino. His hamstring had gone and Jack Simpson had to replace him on 18 minutes. Jack was probably not quite up to the pace of the game and gifted a pass to Saido Mané, who pounced on it and squared to Mo Salah for the Egyptian to shoot past Jefferson Lerma and into the bottom right corner of

Bournemouth's goal on 24 minutes. The game turned further in Liverpool's favour when Lewis Cook tried to clip a ball in the centre circle to Ryan Fraser, and it was intercepted by Virgil van Dijk. That set Mané on his way and he had no trouble in finishing in the bottom right corner, past Aaron Ramsdale on 33 minutes.

The second half was just as entertaining with Ryan Fraser going extremely close to netting his second of the season. He was put through by Philip Billing and chipped over Adrian, only to see James Milner clear off the line. Liverpool also pushed for another goal with Mané going the closest as he rattled the post from some 30 yards. The game intensified as we approached the last quarter. Philip Billing became injured, when substitute Dominic Solanke ran into him. For a while, Bournemouth had to play with 10-men during the last 10 minutes, but Billing hobbled back on to make up the numbers, even if he couldn't run. Bournemouth had already used their three subs with Jack Simpson, Dan Gosling and Dominic Solanke having come on. Jefferson Lerma had been taken off on 80 minutes to protect the midfielder who was just one yellow card away from a two-game suspension. Stanislas had also been subbed by Dominic Solanke on 68 minutes.

The game looked to be going Liverpool's way when a chance popped up for Nathan Aké on 90 minutes. Lewis Cook slipped the ball through to Aké who decided to square it to Callum Wilson. But Wilson got the ball caught under his feet and James Milner and Gomez got back to clear the ball. Looking at the replay Nathan would have just been onside, but the flag went up for Wilson being offside anyway. A final flourish by Liverpool saw Salah cross to Firmino who blazed over the bar.

A 2-1 defeat was a good showing, if not the result that Eddie Howe and Bournemouth fans wanted. At least the team had shown that it could live with the very best away from home, a marked improvement on previous away performances in 2020 up to this point.

The major headaches after the game were much deeper than the thought that the club remained in the bottom three on goal difference. Steve Cook was expected to be out for three or four weeks minimum and with Philip Billing hobbling and Josh King's hamstring there plenty of doubts for the next game. There would be some tired bodies on the physio table in the next week.

The second week in March started well though with good news from the treatment room and the training pitch. Arnold Danjuma and David Brooks were back training with the rest of the team. They might not be expected to start against Crystal Palace in the next match, but they were on course to perhaps be involved.

Just as we started building up to Crystal Palace I

was asked by *The Eagles Beak* to answer some questions before the match. Here is my interview with the Palace Blog:

TEB: What did you make of the game at Selhurst Park earlier in the season?

CC: I thought Bournemouth had been unlucky not to pick up at least a point at Selhurst Park, considering Palace had 10-men for most of the game. It was a close game and I don't think Bournemouth played well enough with their heads. Palace allowed Bournemouth to come on to them and then hit them on the break. Jeffrey Schlupp took his goal very well. Bournemouth had the extra-man and just didn't use that space to their advantage. These games are ones when you really need to pick up something.

TEB: How has the season been for you so far and what are you expecting from the run-in?

CC: Surprise, surprise, it's not been a great season for Bournemouth fans. We seem to get injuries every week and the team is changed so much that they can't get any consistency. It's not that the players aren't trying, but they just get knockback after knockback. We are wondering who has run over half a dozen black cats?
What the team need is a clean sheet. We can't

expect to win games when we are conceding more than one and a half goals a game.

TEB: Bournemouth seem to have had more than their fair share of injuries this season, but do you think there is a reason for this, or is it just one of those seasons?

CC: I am sure the physios have been looking at the data on why so many players are having hamstring injuries, but anything else is down to bad luck. Bournemouth's players are always among the fittest in the league and they are worked hard, but I am not sure if that makes them more prone to injuries. Whatever the case, the injuries have harmed our season. The players mustn't feel sorry for themselves though. They have to get on with it and other players just have to try and step in and do well when they get their chance. If the squad is still not good enough, then questions will be asked about recruitment, because you can't say Bournemouth hasn't spent money.

TEB: Have the fans been critical of Eddie Howe and his management team because of the predicament that you currently find yourselves in?

CC: Most fans don't believe Eddie Howe has been the root cause of the problems that the club has to deal with at this moment. There was a period in January when the mood went a little sour, but very quickly the fans understood that the club needed their support, if they were to mount a good challenge to stay up. Once we knew Eddie was going to stay, the fans responded and the home games have been excellent since the defeat to Watford. Bournemouth has been much harder to beat at home now as Chelsea, Brighton and Aston Villa found out.

TEB: The introduction of VAR this season has not gone to plan so far – what is your view of the system and how it is being used?

CC: Bin it as soon as possible. I don't care if the Premier League says most decisions are correct, it's spoiling the game and just leads to more arguments. I liked the way it was used in the last World Cup but, if they are not prepared to let referees look at monitors, I'm not having it. The referees need to be in charge, not some distant officials in Stockley Park. I think some goals have been disallowed for some petty reasons and the advantage should be with the attacking team, so I'm not a fan of something that tries to reduce the number of goals in games.

TEB: Who will finish top four and bottom three this season?

CC: Liverpool, Man City, Leicester City, Chelsea Brighton & Hove Albion, Aston Villa, Norwich City.

Of course, it could well be Bournemouth that goes down, but we have to be optimistic. If the fans don't think we can stay up we will lose the fight and you have to hope the players feed off the fans' passion and desire to stay up.

TEB: What have you made of Palace this season?

CC: Crystal Palace have done better than expected. I didn't expect Crystal Palace to be in the bottom three but I did expect you to be in the bottom half. Roy Hodgson has the team well set up not to concede goals, and you haven't been so dependent on Wilfried Zaha this season, which I think is a good thing. Jordan Ayew has stepped up in front of goal and nine clean sheets for Vicente Guaita is pretty good going.

TEB: Where do you see Palace and Bournemouth finishing come the end of the season?

CC: Crystal Palace could get into Europe if things go well, but I think the Eagles will land in ninth place. I think all Bournemouth fans would be very pleased if Bournemouth took the 16th or 17th spot this season. It feels like we have been battling relegation all season and it's draining. I just want the players to fight for every point.

TEB: Name one player from each side that will be the ones to watch in this fixture?

CC: James McCarthy is ever present for Crystal Palace this season and is a hard tackler. He doesn't get many headlines, but he makes Palace tick and is good at breaking up moves.

For Bournemouth, it has to be Josh King if he is back. He is such a physical attacker and doesn't get pushed off the ball easily. I just hope he is over his hamstring strain.

TEB: Your prediction?

CC: We have been improving at home and it is average to score two goals at Dean Court per match. What I want to see is Bournemouth also getting a clean sheet and making it a 2-0 win. We need the points!

The chances of AFC Bournemouth beating Crystal Palace might have seemed low to the *Eagles Beak*, but some news that nobody expected would scupper any hope of the fixture being played in March 2020. On 12 March we were told that Mikel Arteta had decided to self-isolate as he was showing signs of having caught the COVID-19 (coronavirus), and

Chelsea player Callum Hudson Odoi was also in self-isolation.

The pandemic had been moving fast and had moved swiftly from Wuhan in Hubei province, China to reach all corners of the world. In the UK, there were 590 confirmed cases on 12 March and by the 13 March it had risen to 798 cases and 10 deaths in the country from the virus. While the UK Government had not banned mass gatherings, the Premier League and football league took matters into their own hands and suspended football. The Premier League would look to restart on 3 April 2020, which meant Bournemouth's games against Crystal Palace at home and Wolverhampton Wanderers away, would have to be rescheduled.

While this might give Bournemouth time for players like Steve Cook to recover from his hamstring problems, there were yet more immediate concerns that Artur Boruc and four employees at AFC Bournemouth were also self-isolating, as they were being tested for COVID-19.

With Eddie Howe cancelling his press conference for the Crystal Palace game, and the football world wondering what would happen next, there was some concern that the whole season could be abandoned. What would that mean for AFC Bournemouth? I thought that the season could be reset as if it were

August 2019. But was this the fairest way to resolve the issue, if the league could not be restarted?

Other considerations were to allow promotions to the Premier League, but no relegations. This would mean a 22-team league with five teams being relegated the next season. What we did learn was that UEFA would suggest that all domestic leagues had to be completed by the end of June 2020 and that the European Championship would be postponed until 2021. I couldn't see how the season could be completed but Asmir Begović, on loan at AC Milan, was clear that a summer feast of football could be possible now that the Euros had been postponed.

The problem was perhaps not only squeezing in fixtures but that the players were under contract only until the end of June at many clubs. The cut-off had to come at the end of June. While Eddie Howe prepared for an improbable match against Newcastle United for 4 April, with the Crystal Palace and Wolves games postponed for a future date, the world was consumed with the spread of COVID-19 and nonsensical panic buying in the shops.

Meanwhile, AFC Bournemouth took the opportunity to release its bad news on its annual results for the financial year ending 30 June 2019. A loss of £32.4m had fans gasping at the accounts and I wrote a piece up about it on the blog.

'The accounts for AFCB make poor reading with a financial loss of £32.4m in the accounting period ending 30 June 2019. This is on top of a loss of £10.9m in the previous financial year. While much of the investment has been spent on player signings, which rose to £94.2m last year compared to £55.8m the year before, it does indicate that the Cherries have spent more than they perhaps should have to be competitive in the Premier League. This kind of spending is unsustainable in the long-term and AFCB are again playing the roulette wheel in my opinion.

'The player and staff wages have risen significantly at £110.9 compared to £101.9m in FY18. The club did not disclose how much money was paid to agents during the period. The income of the club was largely dependent on their league position finish which was 14th and landed the club with £131.1m in FY19 down from £134.9m in FY18. But non-Premier League revenue was virtually stable at £15.5m.

'The club's Chief Executive Neill Blake stressed that £22.6m profit did come into the club shortly after the accounting period closed on player sales, but even that would still show AFCB has been prepared to take a loss of over £10m for the past two seasons to keep its Premier League status.

'What happens if the club goes down to the Championship with a parachute payment and a need to recoup funds with player sales? The club did not reveal whether it is in debt and if so by how much, but most of its assets are on the playing field and we could see many players need to leave if the club is relegated. The only problem is that those market values won't be as high as if the club remains in the top flight.

'Spending big might have kept the club growing, but this season it hasn't resulted in better results. The signing of Dominic Solanke and Philip Billing in the last 12-18 months and the sale of Lys Mousset doesn't bode me with great confidence about recruitment and player sales, even if the purchase of Jack Stacey and Lloyd Kelly and the sale of Tyrone Mings can be considered better decisions. The direction of player spending perhaps needs to change very quickly. That is why the new training complex is vital to bring players through and to reduce the player transfer fees. The model AFCB has worked okay when the big money continues to come in, but it could leave the club having to face the music next season if things don't go according to plan on the pitch. The new stadium idea certainly looks a distant pipe dream with this set of financial results.

*'NB. I was self-isolating at this time having picked up a chest infection and high-temperature. I was over the worst, but I advise others to self-isolate if they feel any flu-like symptoms as soon as they can for the sake of the elderly and those with underlying conditions. We'll beat this. UTCIAD!'*

While I was recuperating, I managed to keep

enough comments to keep the blog going. Keeping things going was also the aim of the Premier League as it moved the resumption date for matches back to 30 April and announced that the season could be extended indefinitely to get games finished. I had my concerns about this, as many players would be out of contract by 30 June. For AFCB alone this would include, Artur Boruc, Charlie Daniels, Simon Francis, Jordon Ibe, and Ryan Fraser, while Harry Wilson's loan period would have expired. Simon Francis said it was not the time to talk about contracts yet, but said he saw his future at AFCB and Bournemouth.

Charlie Daniels was meanwhile making good progress in his recovery since sustaining a dislocated left knee in the Man City game early in the season. He had not only had an operation but had also had stem cell treatment to grow cartilage back around his knee. He then had to spend the couple of weeks of rehabilitation on his back. He was now running on the AlterG running equipment, which meant he could increase the weight on his left knee gradually. He was up to 60 per cent at this time.

# Chapter 10. April – Lockdown

Eddie Howe made the headlines at the end of March as he became the first Premier League manager to take a pay-cut during the COVID-19 outbreak. He was joined by Jason Tindall, Neill Blake and Richard Hughes.

April began with a meeting by the Premier League where it was decided that the season would now no longer be restarted at the beginning of May, it just wasn't going to be possible. The only advice now was that football would be resumed when it was deemed safe to do so. To help lower league clubs, the Premier League brought forward its donation of £125m to lower league clubs in the English Football League and non-league. The Premier League clubs also agreed that their players should take a 30 per cent pay-cut. Some £20m was also donated to the NHS to continue its battle on the front line against COVID-19.

If fans wanted a sign that the authorities still wanted to complete the season's fixture, we heard it on Saturday 4 April when UEFA unblocked the ability of matches to be televised live at 3 pm on Saturdays.

If a tournament-style round of games could be held in June and July the season might get to a finish, but it was still very ambitious, not knowing how the players would feel about the danger to them and how the matches could be staffed by healthcare assistants, if they were still pre-occupied with dealing with COVID-19.

Meanwhile, Simon Francis joined Jordan Henderson and other Premier League captains in forming the #Playerstogether initiative to directly support the NHS with donations that could be made anonymously by players.

Bournemouth's players were in the news for getting back to fitness. Arnaut Danjuma was the main case in point as he admitted he still had a lot to prove on the south coast since his move the previous summer. Chris Mepham and David Brooks were also reported to be close to a return and the numbers for the squad would soon be back towards full strength.

While Easter headed towards us, the club decided to play a re-rum of the West Ham United v AFC Bournemouth match from August 2015, when Bournemouth had their first Premier League win 3-4. The match was streamed on *YouTube* with former Cherry Marc Pugh announcing that he would be watching the game just to see his famous chop on Aaron Creswell again before he scored his goal and Bournemouth's third in what would be a hat-trick day for Callum Wilson.

Callum himself was talking to *SkySports* and indicating that he still had a good chance of making the Euros for England now that they had been postponed a year. I agreed that Callum could find his goal-scoring touch at the right time but first, he would need to see Bournemouth stay up if the season was played out.

AFC Bournemouth along with several other Premier League clubs had furloughed some of their staff in response to the COVID-19 pandemic, but on 14 April 2020, the club reversed its decision to apply for the government's job retention scheme, which would pay 80 per cent of people's earnings each month the pandemic lasted. The statement said that the club had listened to the fans and the criticism aimed at clubs furloughing staff. It was the right call on the publicity side and Bournemouth could now move on from their uneasy position that they had previously put themselves in.

Meanwhile, Eddie Howe was being interviewed by *SkySports* about his time during the crisis and how he was keeping on top of what the players were doing. He seemed very concerned that the club had just nine games to ensure their Premier League status and that all his efforts were currently focused on that.

As fans were still being starved of football, the club decided to pick another match to view from the past. This time it was the historic 1-5 win over Fulham in March 2015 as AFC Bournemouth marched towards the Championship title. This was the Brett Pitman match when he ran half the field to slot away an impressive goal, and Steve Cook also scored an incredible goal with a volley that found the top corner of the goal, from a wide-angle as Bournemouth romped to another famous away win.

Sad news followed that Dickie Dowsett, Bournemouth's former striker, and commercial manager had passed away at the age of 88. I always marvel at AFCB's crest with Dickie's silhouette on the badge. It is like no other club crest and Dickie was one of a kind as a player too, being the sixth-highest all-time scorer for AFCB.

Better news came for the EPL Invitational Tournament. Philip Billing's nimble fingers took him past Southampton's Alex Gunn 4-0 as he progressed to the quarter-finals.

AFCB also gave notice that they would re-show the AFC Bournemouth v Liverpool match from December 2016 which saw Bournemouth's dramatic 4-3 comeback with Nathan Aké pouncing on an injury-time winner.

But the real question fans were intrigued with was how quickly would new games return? I wrote on the blog about the situation on 26 April. "Although talks have been taking place behind closed doors about when the Premier League could return, according to *The Sun* newspaper, I can't see there being anything but big risks if it does return as soon as 8 June, as had been proposed.

"Playing behind closed doors is still going to mean some 250 people being tested each game, and the safety of players, the police and ball boys, etc are still going to be at risk.

"To me, it talks of money being put before the lives of many. We all want football back, but like Georgie Bingham on *TalkSport,* I don't think it can be done safely while social distancing is in place. What choice do the players have in this matter? I suspect none at all. It will be down to the Premier League and Chief Executives or Chairman of each club to say if they can play or not, and there will be pressure put on everybody to go along with it.

'However, this season is completed it will always be a season that has been disrupted and for that reason is not going to be a true reflection of what might have happened, if games had not been postponed. We can pretend that playing behind-closed-doors makes little difference, but we all know it will take some teams more time than others to get a good feeling about that situation. The winners will be those who adapt quickest to this new non-atmosphere football. But there will be a bitter taste for the losers,' I wrote on *Cherry Chimes*.

'Of course, if the Premier League goes ahead there will be mounting pressure from the English football league to play out their remaining games.

How easy will it be to allow all clubs to complete their fixtures? If it is difficult for the Premier League, it is going to be even harder for the lower leagues, who just don't have big operating budgets. Will their safety be as tight as the barriers that will be put in place by the Premier League?

My big worry in all this is that the fans will just have to lump it, whatever is decided. Fans won't be able to travel to games or cheer on their team. Perhaps they will be able to see it on terrestrial TV, but what happens for those TV companies that have exclusive rights? The whole thing is quite a mess and with players contracts running out on 30 June, I wonder how much of the general chatter is more desperation, knowing that the time has pretty much run out to get football back. The Dutch league has already abandoned the season and if more leagues go that way, questions will be asked over the safety of any attempt to try and resurrect the game before social distancing has been removed.'

While AFCB fans soon saw Philip Billing end his ePremier League invitational tournament with a defeat to Brighton's Neal Maupay, the only football to watch was seeing the re-run of AFCB's win over Bolton Wanderers in 2015, which saw the Cherries promoted to the top tier.

As we approached the end of April, there was a growing focus on what was going to happen with football. While talks were said to be going on behind closed doors, Arsenal got their players to come to the training ground to do some individual fitness work. It wasn't long before a few other clubs joined in opening their training grounds – Brighton, West Ham and Spurs followed Arsenal's example, and it led me to ask if AFC Bournemouth would feel forced into asking their players back too?

'This week we have seen the likes of Arsenal, West Ham, Brighton and Spurs all deciding that their players need to start returning to the training grounds. But others like Watford's Chairman have said it is too soon, and the players that can train at their club's training ground are only able to do personal training on their own. Where does this leave AFCB?

'*TalkSport* did a survey on club's positions and with Kings Park closed off to recreation, it doesn't look like AFCB are easily going to get a go-ahead to get back to their training ground. But will other teams gain an advantage by getting back in the groove earlier? They may do and it may make little difference, but once one club looks like they are benefitting, other clubs will want to follow like sheep. I suspect Bournemouth will ask to start-up training again if more than half of the Premier League clubs are doing this.' I said.

'At the end of the day, nobody wants to get left behind, and the league is so competitive that the owners have to be seen to be giving their teams the best chance of having a good finish if the league resumes. Bournemouth might look most closely at the other bottom five clubs. With Brighton and West Ham already looking to start up their training, it may be thought that the Cherries won't want too many others around their league place starting up before them. Yet, the club may be more concerned with the teams they still have to play and how quickly they return, one of which is Spurs.

'Whatever AFCB decides it has to be what is the best decision for them and their players. The club has to see how much training the players are doing in self-isolation and whether they could do more if they are in a big field, not far from their team-mates. Is it psychologically good to be around fellow players? Probably yes, but once players go back, they have to make sure they can do something worthwhile on the training ground, or the players will soon tire of having to go in if they can't train fully as a team.'

While I felt a bit of a lone voice in not wanting the teams to return too early, I was suddenly surprised to see that France had banned football until at least September, virtually ending any chance of the football season resuming there. The FIFA's Chief Medical Officer then warned the Premier League of the dangers of trying to restart too soon. Simon Jordan, ex-Crystal Palace owner, and Chairman, on *TalkSport* went even further arguing that clubs would be risking corporate manslaughter if they made their players play and one of them or their family caught COVID-19 and died from it.

# Chapter 11. May – Project Restart

By the start of May the noise about Project Restart, as the media liked to call the resumption of the Premier League, was gathering pace. The clubs met to try and formulate a way forward, with the question of neutral venues at the top of the agenda. While up to 10 such stadiums might be required, there was another suggestion of using St George's Park, the national training complex, as the perfect venue to host all the games.

I wrote about the subject on 2 May. 'I admire the thought now going into project restart for the Premier League. Alan Brazil on *TalkSport* came up with an idea that sounds pretty good of using the national St George's Park, where there are 13 outdoor pitches and a hotel.

'I think wherever games are played it will be difficult, but a complex like St George's Park does allow for a certain amount of containment for players and staff - almost like a mini-village, where players are put almost into a World Cup kind of setting. What makes it hard for me is the number of games that need to be played, and would the league expect teams to come and go when their fixtures are on, then go back, or could they all be based nearby? The problem of travel is going to crop up if there are several neutral venues but if the Premier League could quarantine a big venue, and surrounding area, it would kind of be a fairly closed shop to people coming and going,' I said.

But it wasn't long before further news of some clubs being willing to finish the season began to surface, with the proviso that there was no relegation. I wasn't sure if the season could be completed with such a stance taken by some clubs, but the pressure was on for a solution, as the clock was ticking.

There was a worry from PFA Chief Executive, Gordon Taylor, that the games would have to be shorter than 90 minutes if the league did restart. The only thing was to be fair to all teams the previous game would have to be re-evaluated, by seeing what the scores were in these games after 60-minutes. The media studied the differences that this would make and was surprised by how the table would look. I was shocked to see that while Liverpool would still be way ahead, it would mean some drastic changes in league positions.

The amazing fact for Bournemouth fans is that we would suddenly see the side in mid-table, in 14th, on

32 points, six points above the relegation zone and with a much better chance of survival. But crazily the bottom three would consist of Wolves, who would see 17 points knocked off of their total.'

Sadly, the idea didn't have any legs and it looked like if Bournemouth were going to escape the trap door, they would have to do it from where they were in the table now, 18th, and matches would be of 90 minutes duration, not 60 minutes long.

The atmosphere was starting to turn sour as the Premier League voiced its own opinion on the bottom clubs who were thinking of voting against a resumption because they disliked neutral venues.

'It appears several clubs, Aston Villa, Norwich and Brighton, for example, have been less than keen on playing the remaining matches of this season at neutral venues, which I think is understandable as teams in the bottom half have found points hard to come by. Home advantage is a big help with the familiarity of stadiums,' I blogged.

However, the Premier League was having none of it. They said, that if the bottom clubs vote against their dream Project Restart they'll relegate the bottom three with a vote by the other clubs. I was in no doubt what I thought of the way the Premier League was acting. The threatening behaviour was uncalled for and it got me shouting.

'The Premier League is stamping its feet and is lobbying the government to get them onside, so it can make its money and get worldwide coverage of the remaining games as a big spectacle, raising the profile of the league even higher. It doesn't care about the fans not being able to attend the games. It doesn't care which teams are relegated, as all the big clubs are well and truly safe. It just wants to see Liverpool gain the title that they deserve and tie up all the loose ends, on relegation and European places, so that their precious league can be completed.' I said.

I was not asking for the season to be abandoned if the games could be played out safely. But every club has its priorities and getting an agreement would be difficult. I wrote on the blog on 4 May, 'Frankly, if there is no relegation I don't see why the Premier League needs to play to a finish this season. The places for financial payments could be taken from the positions now. It would then be up to the Premier League if they would be willing to expand the league by accepting promoted sides, although this would affect the numbers of teams in the Championship and Leagues One and Two – would they also promote and relegate sides from all the English football leagues?'

The uncertainty of everything was getting so frustrating. 'At least we will know in June whether the whole idea of Project Restart is something that everyone has got behind, or if the clubs can just start preparing for a hopeful 2020-21 season, which has to be the best way forward, in my opinion, to give clubs a more achievable goal. Clubs need time to plan for their futures without being left on tenterhooks as they are being asked to do at present.

The one good thing I could see about a possible resumption was to see the return of David Brooks, even if this would only be via an online stream. I summarised that 'We have not seen David Brooks since the pre-season friendly with Brentford at Griffin Park on 27 July 2019. It is almost a year and I wonder just how many goals David would have scored in that time if he had been available. He has had a worthy deputy in Harry Wilson, but there is something majestic about David Brooks playing and AFCB fans need to see him develop.

'While I am not overly confident that AFCB will avoid relegation, with David Brooks on top form they do have a better chance of survival. If Brooks can just show that he is the intelligent player that we have seen in his first season at AFCB, Bournemouth will see that they have more attacking verve in the last third. I don't want to put pressure on Brooks and I think Eddie Howe will also play down his return to some extent, but the manager will know more than most that. A top-firing David Brooks will light up the Premier League, and that will improve Bournemouth's hopes of staying there.'

One club that was looking safer than the Cherries was the Saints. Bournemouth had decided to cherry-pick the game against the Saints at St Mary's from earlier in the season. 'Looking at the Cherries' 'repicked' game this week, it is great that our fans finally have a game to truly enjoy, as it has been a long time in coming to beat the Saints at their ground. St Mary's simply hasn't been a happy hunting ground until this season, but one look at the current table shows that the Saints have shown much more resolve than AFCB to get out of trouble in 2019-20.'

I continued, 'Things were so different in September 2019, when Bournemouth enjoyed a 1-3 win over Southampton and the season looked like it was on course for being a good one for AFCB. Many mistakes were made after that game and the inconsistency in front of goal, and the failure to keep hardly any clean sheets took away the early pleasure of wins against Everton and Southampton.

The hosting of away games was something most fans were now expecting or at least neutral grounds but, by mid-June, the idea of neutral grounds had been binned. 'The Premier League looks like it will have to admit defeat over its insistence of playing out the remainder of the season at neutral grounds. Talks between the police, the Premier League and the government have resulted in more positive assurances that games can be played behind closed doors at all of the 20 Premier League grounds, reported *TalkSport* if Project Restart gets up and running.

*The Daily Mail* then asked if I would comment on

Project Restart, so I gave them the following answers to their questions.

*Daily Mail*: Should the season be null and void? If so, why?

CC: 'Null and void would be best now. Player safety and the people who have to be at any behind closed doors match are still not going to be 100 per cent safe.'

*Daily Mail*: Do you think it should be played out when possible but with no relegation?

CC: 'No. It would be best to move on to the 2020-21 season. Start things from as they were in August 2019. If clubs have nothing to play for, apart from the European places, the incentive for the lower teams is only going to be about four or five places higher or lower than where they are now.'

*Daily Mail*: Should players just crack on with it or are they right to be worried about returning to action?

CC: 'They are right to be worried. I wouldn't want to take the risk. Why should they feel any different from the rest of us? The Premier League is putting money and their TV contracts ahead of common sense. Plan for next season and get proper safety measures in place to have a more realistic aim of starting at the end of this year or waiting for the vaccine.'

While a resumption in England for football still looked at least a month away, the games had begun again in Germany. They were not, of course, in front of a stadium full of people, but it was football of sorts. I captured the excitement, before the first games, that would again bring football to our screens. 'While the Premier League still has some squabbles to sort out, the Bundesliga in Germany is firing up its resumption this weekend. Bayern Munich will probably wrap up another title, but at the bottom, it is a fight for survival for Paderborn, Werder Bremen and Düsseldorf. UK fans might not have a favourite football team in Germany, but there will probably be quite a few of us logging on to see just how close to normal these games are.'

While looking to the continent for inspiration, there was also a link between Bournemouth and a player in Spain. The only probable catch was that another relegation candidate was also keen on the player. 'The race to stay in the Premier League has no doubt become a little hotter between AFCB and Brighton & Hove Albion with both clubs said to be tracking Monchu, a 20-year-old Barcelona B player. Monchu is a midfielder who is the highest scorer this season in the Barcelona B team, and AFCB has been tracking him for the last three years, according to *FootballEspana*.

Closer to home AFC Bournemouth had been welcoming to a couple of former players from Newcastle United and Liverpool. Adam Lallana and Matt Ritchie had been training at Kings Park.

'Adam Lallana, 30, was good enough to have a clause in his contract when he signed for Southampton that gave AFCB some funds when he was sold from Southampton to Liverpool, and the fact that he has been in conversation with AFCB, albeit with Alan Connell and the U18s, I do think it puts AFCB in a favourable position to pick Adam up this summer when he ends his playing time at Anfield,' I said.

Bournemouth fans were treated to another of the repicked games, but this time it was the other side of the city of Liverpool. Yes, a replay of the AFCB 3 v 3 Everton comeback of 2015-16. Do you remember this game?

Many fans will have watched the Everton repicked game last night in the 2015-16 season with Funes Mori and Lukaku giving Everton a 2-0 half-time lead, before Adam Smith and Junior Stanislas hit back in the last 10 minutes of normal time to make it 2-2. It looked all over then when Ross Barkley made it 2-3 in extra-time, but Bournemouth just never let up in that game and Junior Stanislas denied an Everton win with a 90+8 minute equaliser.

The match reminded me of everything we are missing. Without a crowd to cheer and jeer at the officials and opposition, football wasn't quite as enjoyable. I summed it up on the blog 'Those comebacks became second nature to the Cherries in the early Premier League days. What we would give for a few turnarounds in games like that today. But what makes a good comeback? This game was a special one not because it was against a big named team, and it wasn't even a derby. But there was a gritted feeling about the game which transmits through the crowd and that atmosphere generates the magic.'

We seemed a long way away from the magic. Instead we were wondering whether the Premier League's Project Restart should indeed be given the legs to run. COVID-19 testing for players had begun, but the results were not all good.

'The fact that six Premier league players and staff proved positive for COVID-19 symptoms last weekend has already put doubts in some players' minds if they want to go back to training. Jamie Redknapp has said on *SkySports* that more players will quit training, like Troy Deeney and N'Golo Kanté. The integrity of any competition is therefore shattered, and it's hard to see the end of the Premier League season being anything more than a fudge solution,' I said.

While fans and players might wonder how much say they would have about events as they were played out, I just hoped that the final decisions of the players would be respected if they didn't want to take to the field.

'At the moment it all seems too soon and high risk. Things may look better in a month or we could get the start of the second wave of coronavirus. It all feels like an experiment at the moment, but whether there is a good safety net in place is hard to see. Players are going to have to go with their gut instinct and I only hope that fans will respect the decisions of individual players who will surely have worries about pulling out. Players need more big stars to come out and say if they are unsure about training. It would take the pressure off of others who may feel vulnerable if they come out and say they don't feel comfortable about playing. The mental health staff at clubs have their work cut out in the next few weeks,' I commented.

While players grappled with their risk to themselves and family, the fans also had reason to get thinking when the topic of refunds for the outstanding games was mentioned. Did fans want refunds or, like Walsall fans, would they donate these funds to the club?

I gave the matter some coverage on the blog 'I was thinking myself about whether I wanted to see AFCB offer a refund on the home games that are left this season, or whether they would offer something in exchange for the money paid for games that have yet to be played next season. Then I saw that the *BBC* had a news story on Saturday on how some fans of lower league club fans were needed to support their clubs by donating the money they had paid for remaining games, just to help keep their clubs afloat.'

Bournemouth's situation was very different from those in the lower leagues. Most fans who commented thought it only right that the club refund the fans and many wondered why they hadn't done it already. 'AFCB are not about to go under, but they will no doubt be grateful for any revenue they can hold on to because their outgoings have been greater than income for the last few years. I suppose you can blame this on the wages they are offering to players and some of the high transfer and agent fees. It is the environment in which they operate, although perhaps other clubs can manage their finances better, especially when they have bigger fanbases.'

In the background, COVID-19 was very much still dominating everything in the world, even if some countries had come fully out of lockdown. As if we needed a reminder that we needed to keep washing our hands and 'Staying Alert' as the new Government slogan went. A Bournemouth player tested positive for COVID 19. It turned out to be goalkeeper Aaron Ramsdale.

I was shocked but 'The fact that an AFCB player has tested positive for COVID-19 tells us that this virus is still all around us and it doesn't respect what you do or who you are. Anyone can catch the coronavirus and I imagine the cleaning around Dean

Court has gone into overdrive since the learning of this second batch of tests has picked out a Bournemouth player, who may not even have thought that he was carrying the virus.'

This was all a balancing act of risk and progressing with preparation for the restart. Things could quickly change though and the news that players were still as vulnerable as anyone else was another reminder about the dangers of this potentially killer virus.

I gave some thought to what kind of risk was acceptable for the football authorities. Were two positive tests out of 9996 a good thing? 'It is difficult to know how the authorities feel about what is acceptable for football to go ahead if a small number of players are still picking up symptoms and having positive tests. While we may be a month away from the action of a match day, perhaps this is acceptable, but once we get into June, who wants to play if there is a sudden spout of cases?

The mood was lifted a bit by AFC Bournemouth announcing that they would be using a new kit for the games left in the season. *Mansion88*'s contract was up at the end of May and it was not going to be renewed. Bournemouth would play without sponsors on their shirts for the last nine games and a bright yellow training kit was the first new strip we would see. Callum Wilson said that the team would play like Brazil in the new yellow shirts – we could only hope that would be true.

Contact training was now given permission and Bournemouth started training as much in their empty stadium as on the training pitches. They were trying to get whatever advantage they could by getting used to playing in an empty stadium for when football resumed.

# Chapter 12. June – Football returns

The Premier League would resume in June and the fans were supposed to be thrilled that there would be some 92 games and 33 of them would be free to air. As a season ticket holder who now knew he might not see many of Bournemouth's remaining games in the Premier League, it was short change when I previously had five home matches that I could have attended out of the last nine games. But COVID-19 had robbed supporters of the full football experience.

This is how it was going to be. I was asked by *BTSport* if I'd like to do a video of a Bournemouth supporter celebrating a goal and going mad, so they could use it as part of their trailers they wanted to run when football returned. I didn't feel that joyous about what had been happening over the last few months and didn't feel like I wanted to take part in celebrating football's return.

The *Observer* and *Guardian* asked me to write some text about the resumption of the Premier League though and I did give them my thoughts.

*Observer*: The season is about to resume - how

are you feeling about your side's prospects on the pitch? Is your squad in good shape for the run-in, or not? How do you see it going?

CC: AFC Bournemouth's prospects have improved a lot since March with the return of Steve Cook and David Brooks in particular. It has also been good to hear that Liverpool has allowed Harry Wilson to play past 30 June for us. It is going to be a tough run-in, with four of the top six to play, and to try and stay up. Bournemouth will battle and I can see the team causing a few shocks. Whether it will be enough to keep them up is the question. I have a feeling we may just scrape home to safety.

*Observer*: Was it the right decision to restart the season?

CC: The decision looks better now, while a few players are being found positive for COVID-19. But it looks very much that the restart is all about money. The fans won't be able to go to stadiums and they will only see a third of the games free on TV. I would have abandoned the season on safety grounds, even if it did mean automatic relegation for AFC Bournemouth.

*Observer*: What have you missed most about football during lockdown? (Could be something about your club, or more generally - something about the fan experience/media, etc)

CC: Not meeting up with other fans is the biggest miss. You have a routine when you go to games and we miss all that as well. You also miss seeing goals and that thrill of your team winning.

*Observer*: And what have you missed least?

CC: At least we have not been talking about VAR for the last couple of months. I haven't missed that at all and I hope something is done for the following season on VAR because it's been a shambles.

*Observer*: What has lockdown taught you about your club? (It could be something positive and/or negative - for instance the club's positive community work/NHS food deliveries/charity work - or the squad's negative behaviour / lockdown-breaking, or misuse of taxpayers' money, etc)

CC: Just that the players want to stay up. They are dedicated and look focused on the job they need to do now. I'm optimistic that they can still do it and with some novel haircuts!

*Observer*: And finally, some predictions - please

could you give us the top four in order, the bottom three in order, and your club's finishing position?

CC: 1. Liverpool, 2. Man City, 3. Leicester, 4. Chelsea
18. Brighton & Hove Albion 19. Aston Villa 20. Norwich City

While we were progressing towards the restart, most events seemed to be happening behind closed doors, AFC Bournemouth were said to be having a friendly match on 10 June, but we didn't know who against.

Preparations were also being done with players. Harry Wilson signed a new extended loan contract until the end of the season. Diego Rico was explaining to that the Spanish press that he was unsure about his future and that anything could happen, despite having two years remaining on his Bournemouth contract.

One player whose contract AFC Bournemouth had been battling with all season was Ryan Fraser. The winger was unlikely to play again I felt, since news broke that he was likely to reject a short extension past 30 June. It was a good job that Bournemouth had secured Harry Wilson for a few more weeks past the end of June, at least he wanted to play for Bournemouth.

It was clear that football was soon to be returning

when the club released what it termed its 'final Cherries repicked game', the 0-5 win against Brighton in 2018-19. Getting us into a goal frenzy was fine, as long as something like those special days could be replicated in the coming games.

Eddie Howe was himself getting ready for the restart and gave an open interview on *AFCBTV* in which he outlined how he thought games would be in the dramatic end to the season. He expressed that many of the games in Germany had been possession-based and a bit slower tempo without the crowds and he expected things to follow suit in England.

One good vote of confidence came from the *TalkSport* supercomputer that predicted a finish of 17$^{th}$ for the Cherries. We'd soon see if this computer was as visionary as Nostradamus.

One thing that nobody saw coming was the departure of Marc Pugh from QPR. The former Cherry had been playing for the Championship side but would trigger a contract extension for another year if he played another game, which QPR couldn't afford. So, the 33-year old was headed home and I wondered if he could form part of the backroom staff at AFCB, as he would be great to have around to inspire the younger professionals.

The restart was about new things though. We were reminded of that with the release of UMBRO's new home kit for the Cherries. It was a splendid shirt that had fans buzzing. I wrote about it on 16 June on the blog. 'The shirt has been a big departure from the typical red and black stripes, by having them broken up and displaced with a powder effect over the top, which looks particularly striking with the new *Vitality* sponsor logo at the front.'

One player who wouldn't be wearing the new strip was Ryan Fraser who didn't sign a temporary extension to his contract. Eddie Howe reported that the player would not play again for AFC Bournemouth with his contract ending on 30 June. Fraser didn't want to risk being injured which would stop a free transfer to another club in the summer.

With Fraser out of the squad, it was time to concentrate on preparing for Crystal Palace. Eddie Howe said that the players had trained well and are eager to play and to move out of the bottom three. He picked the following side: Ramsdale, Stacey, S Cook, Ake, A Smith, H Wilson, Brooks, Lerma, L Cook, King and C Wilson.

It didn't look a bad team on paper but again Eddie hadn't gone with a recognised left-back and Philip Billing was injured, so it wasn't quite full strength. Everyone was pleased that David Brooks was back and he was easily the best player for Bournemouth on the night. Sadly, he could only look on for much of the game though and wonder why his team-mates weren't doing better. Crystal Palace raced into a 0-2 lead on 23 minutes with Luka Milivojević smashing in a free kick in the top corner after 12 minutes, and

Jordan Ayew ran rings around Adam Smith to make it two goals to the Eagles before half-time.

Eddie Howe put Danjuma on for the start of the second half, and Bournemouth's number 14 showed moments of trickery. However, there was only one attempt on goal from Nathan Aké and Bournemouth fell to their 17$^{th}$ defeat of the season. Worse still, Josh King was on the end of a follow-through challenge form Gary Cahill which would rule him out for at least the next game.

The Cherries remained in the bottom three despite Norwich and West Ham losing, and Aston Villa and Watford getting a point. It was a missed chance with only Brighton, of the bottom six, picking up three points by beating Arsenal and increasing their gap to five points above the relegation zone.

Eddie Howe simply stated that the first goal had killed off Bournemouth. The players had not been able to respond. Crystal Palace are not the team you want to go behind to, as they defend deep and leave no gaps. The game slipped away all too quickly and Palace had easily picked their way through Bournemouth's midfield and defence.

But Bournemouth had to get over the stigma of defeat quickly, because Wolverhampton Wanderers would be next, in four days. There was no throwing in the towel, but the task had just become even harder with eight games to go.

If the pressure was too much for the lads against

Crystal Palace, it was ramped up even more for the Wolves game who had dispatched fellow strugglers West Ham United 0-3 in their last game. Bournemouth used their home shirt with white shorts and socks, as they had done the last time they had won at Molineux. Walking down from a hospitality suite and down the main stand, the players came onto the pitch in a bit of a heatwave at 29°C on a summer Wednesday evening.

What we were hoping for was a massive improvement in energy and creativity. While Eddie brought in Philip Billing and Junior Stanislas for Josh King and Harry Wilson, the rest of the side was unchanged from the Palace defeat. The only problem was that the team was not any more productive in goal attempts and while the team got to half-time at 0-0, it was hard to see how Bournemouth would score. Even a draw would have seen Bournemouth rise out of the bottom three and ahead of West Ham, who had lost 2-0 to Spurs the night before. So, at half-time, it was good to be on level terms with Wolves.

By the start of the second half though, things started to unravel. Philip Billing picked up a dead leg and had to be subbed for Dan Gosling. Callum Wilson had been carded and would miss the next two Bournemouth games. Worse still Adama Traoré was having a blinder. If he wasn't running through the middle of our players, he was rounding Adam Smith on Wolves right side and crossing for Raúl Jimenéz to head in on 60 minutes, timing his run to get in between Jack Stacey and Steve Cook.

We had heard all week how Bournemouth were practising how to break down stubborn defences. They had another such challenge now and although Danjuma, Solanke and Harry Wilson entered the fray as well as Lloyd Kelly, Bournemouth didn't register one shot on target. It was another three points lost in a tight game and Eddie Howe had little to say other than 'the run of results we've been on at the moment has been very difficult to take. We look back and we'll be kicking ourselves that we didn't get at least a draw. There was very little in the game, I thought the lads gave everything to a really good defensive performance. The one moment cost us and we're kicking ourselves really.'

The goal that Wolves scored was a carbon copy of the goal that Jimenéz had scored against West Ham only a few days before. Again, it had been supplied by a Traoré cross and scored by Wolves' top scorer. Bournemouth's players must have watched the goal that was scored against West Ham and must have been warned that this was the main supply route for Wolves, but when the moment came, they could do nothing to stop the ball from hitting the back of the net. No wonder Eddie Howe said his team had been kicking themselves.

The match would also see Callum Wilson miss the

next two games for his 10th yellow card and Philip Billing had a dead leg problem that would also make him a doubt for the next game. But it was the lack of creativity in the team that caused fans to wonder whether AFC Bournemouth had any chance of staying up now. They didn't have a shot on target against Wolves.

A few days after the Wolves game, Bournemouth announced that Jermain Defoe, Ryan Fraser and Jordon Ibe were among players to be released on free transfers by the club at the end of June. Artur Boruc, Simon Francis, Charlie Daniels and Andrew Surman signed contract extensions, until the end of the season, along with Brad Smith who was on loan at Cardiff City.

Eddie Howe was reflecting about the Wolves defeat and tried to remind the press that many of his players had not played that much football. Philip Billing, Arnaut Danjuma, Junior Stanislas, Steve Cook and David Brooks had returned from injuries during the lockdown period, and for them, it was hard to get themselves going in the first two games back. We could only hope that by the third game the players would feel more in the groove to get some points.

The team had been lucky in that only Brighton had picked up more than a point among the bottom six in the two games since the league had restarted. West Ham United and Norwich City, like Bournemouth, had added nothing to their total and Aston Villa and

Watford had only added a point. Southampton did the Cherries a huge favour by beating Watford 1-3 away, two days before Bournemouth would take on Newcastle United in the third match in Bournemouth's fixtures since the restart. A win would lift Bournemouth out of the relegation zone, so it was another big match for the fans to watch. The pressure was on now, with seven games to go. The Newcastle match seemed like a must-win game with the difficult fixtures ahead for the Cherries. The question was, could the players deal with the pressure and finally perform well?

# Chapter 13. July – No way back?

The 1 July was a match day for Bournemouth. All the other games this week had been favourable for the Cherries who now stood a great chance of opening up a gap on other strugglers if they could overcome Newcastle Utd, who were lying in 14$^{th}$ place. The fans knew that this game was a must-win, as no points from the last two games, there wouldn't be a better chance of picking up points and climbing out of the bottom three.

Eddie Howe made four changes to the starting line-up. Callum Wilson was banned for the game and Howe went with Dominic Solanke upfront along with the returning Josh King. Arnaut Danjuma started on the left-wing and Lloyd Kelly was given his first Premier League start. Philip Billing was okay to start having had a dead leg the week before, so Lewis Cook moved to the bench, along with Junior Stanislas and Jack Stacey.

Steve Bruce's side was a long way from home, but they had no problems in starting well in their bright orange kit. Bournemouth made a mess of playing out from the back in the first five minutes. Lerma lost control of the ball and Saint-Maximin slipped a ball through to Dwight Gayle to give the Toon the early lead. The goal clearly affected the Bournemouth players and they soon found themselves in deeper trouble.

Saint-Maximin dribbled his way around Adam Smith like he wasn't there, and David Brooks didn't provide much cover. The pull-back found Sean Longstaff who thumped the ball into the roof of the net on half an hour.

It was like the Crystal Palace game all over again. Bournemouth's players had frozen on a night when they could ill afford any slip-up. While Lewis Cook replaced Billing at the start of the second half, there was not much happening for the Cherries. Only David Brooks looked anything like sharp.

Miguel Almirón made it 0-3 to the visitors when he latched on to another pass from Saint-Maximin, lashing the ball past Aké and Ramsdale to find the top corner. Lazaro then completed the demolition when he came on to replace Saint-Maximin. He found space on the left and beat Ramsdale to make it 0-4 on 77 minutes. It took Bournemouth 93 minutes to get a shot on goal and then Dan Gosling scored the consolation goal to leave Bournemouth a 1-4 defeat and second bottom in the table.

Eddie Howe was again hurt by the result and felt

the players lacked zip. They hadn't improved at playing in an empty stadium and now with West Ham United winning against Chelsea, Bournemouth looked in a more perilous the position.

There was little to be happy about with Bournemouth rooted in the bottom two and saddled with an awful string of results. The club did its best to raise spirits in releasing the new turquoise away strip, which had a mixed reaction on social media. I thought it looked okay, with a splosh of darker blue running diagonally across the shirt. Of course, we'd all like the new kit if the team could win their next away game in it.

The press conference for Eddie Howe before the Manchester United game was an eye-opener on how much pressure the team was now under. Steve Cook had spoken out on social media saying that they played like schoolboys against Newcastle. Eddie Howe said such comments did not help the team and that he preferred such matters to be kept in-house. We wondered if Steve Cook would be dropped after his comments and for the way he performed against Newcastle himself.

Eddie said there were some players carrying knocks before the Manchester United game, but wouldn't say who they were. He commented that they were in a similar position to when they needed to get a result away at Chelsea in December.

Everyone had written Bournemouth off, but the team often fights back well when it is at its lowest point.

Eddie was asked about whether he would be considering his position, but he said such questions were redundant at the moment. He was only concerned with getting the best from his players. Still, 16 defeats in the last 21 matches equalled relegation form and he knew it.

I spoke with the *Old Trafford Faithful* blog before the match to see how confident the Manchester United fans were.

CC: Are you surprised that Anthony Martial has suddenly hit the sweet spot in his scoring having had the first hat-trick for Man Utd in an absolute age?

OTF: I'll be honest, I am. I'm not the biggest Anthony Martial fan out there, though I appreciate he's a super-talented young man. Inconsistency has hampered his growth over the last few seasons, but now with a manager in place who believes in him, perhaps he can take his game to that next level? I'm more than happy to be proven wrong!

CC: Marcus Rashford is the best role model in English football at the moment. But how has he done since the restart on the football field?

OTF: He's struggled, though we have to remember

he was suffering from a pretty serious back injury before lockdown. I'm happy to give him another couple of weeks to get back up to speed before judging him too harshly, though!

CC: What would be a success for Ole Gunnar Solskjaer this season – FA Cup winners and fifth place? And is it good that the press has stopped talking about him losing his job?

OTF: I'm pleased that the press is off his back for now, because I genuinely believe he has been the best manager we've had since Sir Alex Ferguson.

To me, it's all about trophies. An FA Cup win would be lovely, while I give us a great shot in the Europa League, too. A top-four finish would be the icing on the cake as Champions League football is key when it comes to attracting those big-name signings.

CC: Do you expect Man Utd to make a move for either Josh King or David Brooks this summer?

OTF: I think the Josh King boat has probably sailed. I said it at the time, but there were worse options available in January than the former United man.

As for David Brooks, I love watching him operate. It's a shame that injury has wrecked his season because he was outstanding last term. He fits the player-profile that Solskjaer had shown a preference towards. He'd be pretty pricey, but it's a deal I'd fully get behind.

CC: Where do Man Utd need to strengthen to become a challenger for the Premier League title next time around?

OTF: United need a world-class right-winger, another centre-half and some more depth in midfield - hence why I like the possibility of the versatile Brooks joining.

CC: What do you think of how Bournemouth has performed this season and their league position?

OTF: I, like all Bournemouth fans I'm sure, are feeling pretty disappointed. The results and overall displays haven't been anywhere near the level I expected - though I appreciate injuries and behind-closed-doors situations (Ryan Fraser) haven't helped...
It's sad because I love Eddie Howe and the work he is doing down there. I just hope Bournemouth stay up!

CC: Which three teams do you think will go down?

OTF: I think Villa and Norwich are already gone. West Ham, Watford and Bournemouth are all in danger of finishing 18th and going down. I think it'll be Watford as the other two have so much quality in their ranks, but right now it's a toss-up...

CC: Bournemouth managed to beat Man Utd at Dean Court this season, so is this far from a gimme for Man Utd at Old Trafford, despite AFCB's recent poor away form?

OTF: There must be something in those south coast waters as we always struggle down there! Jokes aside, I feel far more comfortable with this game being at home, and we're playing pretty well right now.

No game is a gimme, and United will have to perform, but I'm hopeful we can pick up all three points here, sorry folks!

CC: How would you expect Man Utd to line up for this game?

OTF: As strong as we can. We need to win every single fixture to give ourselves the best shot at finishing in the top four.

David de Gea, Aaron Wan-Bissaka, Victor Lindelof,

Harry Maguire, Luke Shaw, Nemanja Matic, Paul Pogba, Bruno Fernandes, Mason Greenwood, Marcus Rashford, Anthony Martial.

That's about as good as it gets for us right now, though that front five must be pretty scary for any opposing side!

CC: How many do you think Man Utd should win by?

OTF: Two? Three. I'll go for a 3-1 United win...

Well, goals were on the cards with Bournemouth having trouble keeping a clean sheet and about to go up against the most in-form team of the division. We expected changes to the line-up and Eddie Howe didn't disappoint. What we didn't expect was for Lloyd Kelly to start at centre-back. Steve Cook had tweaked his hamstring and was not available. Worse still, Chris Mepham had travelled with the team, but he had not felt right and had to sit the game out. Junior Stanislas was given a start on the left-wing and Lewis Cook replaced Philip Billing in midfield. Diego Rico also came back into the side at left-back allowing Adam Smith to move over to his more customary right-back position. Bournemouth still had to look around to get nine players on the bench and Mark

Travers took up the last sub's space, joining Artur Boruc to make a third keeper.

Preparations might have gone better. Still Bournemouth made their best start since the restart of the games. Adam Smith put in a cross and it fell out to Junior Stanislas. Junior saw his first shot blocked and received the ball again, nutmegging Harry Maguire on the left side of the box, before beating De Gea at his near post. Bournemouth were 0-1 up in the first 15 minutes.

At this rate, we could get to like the new blue away kit, which was having its first outing. The prospect of a win didn't last long though. Mason Greenwood lashed a fierce shot past Ramsdale, before the half-hour with the Bournemouth defence overly stretched.

While the resistance had been broken, Bournemouth fans didn't expect to be 3-1 down by half-time. The goals just kept coming as Adam Smith made a handball in the box and Marcus Rashford scored from the spot. Then Anthony Martial picked out the top corner with a spectacular bending drive, in added time, at the end of the first half.

Eddie Howe must have said some good words of encouragement at half-time, as Bournemouth came out raging with a hunger to get back in the game. Harry Maguire lost the ball with a bad pass and Solanke strode away like he was going to slip in his first Premier League goal. But he lost control with challenges all around him. The ball broke to Lewis Cook who smacked a powerful drive that De Gea did well to keep out. Then Danjuma managed to only hit the post from a tight angle, as he followed up.

Bournemouth fans might have thought the chance had gone, but United still had trouble playing out from the back and a questionable handball by Eric Bailly gave Josh King the opportunity to bring the score back to 3-2 from the penalty spot.

Another chance for Danjuma saw him race down the right side and score, but VAR ruled the goal out just as we thought Bournemouth were back on level terms. Our disappointment was doubled moments later when Greenwood made it 4-2 on 54 minutes. That was still not the end of the goals. A foul by Lloyd Kelly gave Fernandes the chance to snap a free kick in past Ramsdale on 59 minutes. Bournemouth had suddenly fallen 5-2 down with any hope of a point having gone.

The thing that Bournemouth fans could take from the game was that their players had tried. They had given it a go and played with far more fight than in the previous four matches. Still, Eddie Howe could hardly be pleased with a 5-2 defeat, even if his team has performed.

With Watford beating Norwich 2-1 at Vicarage Road the following Tuesday night, Bournemouth would have to take on Spurs on Thursday now four points adrift of safety. Relegation was not so much as

# NO WAY BACK?

a possibility but expected now with the remaining fixtures Bournemouth had to play.

Eddie was honest after the match and was most disappointed with the first goal against Bournemouth at Old Trafford that gave Manchester United a foothold in the game. He was pleased that the team created chances and looked razor-sharp at times, but Eddie said Man United had incredible finishing. That is why he wanted Bournemouth to stay in this league, as he wanted to play the best teams.

For a long period of the game, Bournemouth would be a threat, but Eddie said it would be foolish to say the team was making progress, conceding five goals. Still some aspects of the game were better in the Man United match. Like some of the individual performances. Still, 'As a collective, it still wasn't good enough,' said Eddie.

Steve Cook and Chris Mepham's absence from the team probably didn't help the defence. They were late injuries the day before the game and on the day of the game, but putting Lloyd Kelly in at centre-back did show how talented Lloyd is.

Eddie faced some more difficult questions ahead of the visit of Tottenham, with games running out fast. He decided that Kelly would start again in central defence, as Steve Cook still wasn't injury-free. Dominic Solanke was dropped to the bench to allow the return of Callum Wilson, after his two-match suspension. Meanwhile, Dan Gosling replaced Lewis Cook in central midfield.

Bournemouth started a bit haphazardly giving away a few free kicks, but they soon warmed to the task. An early bit of luck saw Josh King fall into Harry Kane at a corner and while VAR checked for a possible penalty for Spurs, the decision went the Cherries way.

Serge Aurier was Tottenham's provider and he kept getting down the right-wing. But Gosling was marshalling the midfield and Bournemouth started to create problems for Tottenham. While Sissoko and Lerma wanted to get into a bit of a skirmish. Junior Stanislas registered the only shot on target right at the end of the first half, when he turned sharply and drilled a low shot that Lloris turned around the post.

Tottenham tried to get more attacks going second half, substituting Steven Bergwijn and Giovani Lo Celso, and putting on Son Heung-Min and Tanguy Ndombele. Lerma gave away a free kick on the edge of the box which Harry Kane lined up, but his shot struck Adam Smith in the stomach. Bournemouth then had a penalty claim when Jan Vertonghen had taken Callum Wilson down, but VAR didn't award a penalty.

A few minutes later Adam Smith was concussed, after a head collision with Ben Davies. Jack Stacey had to replace Adam Smith, who was stretchered off. Harry Wilson also came on soon after to replace

David Brooks. I'd hoped it would have been Danjuma coming on for his directness.

After Kelly made a great clearance off the six-yard box, Lucas Moura came on and the Spurs attacks became more frequent. Then, Bournemouth thought they had the lead. Callum Wilson sent Stanislas down the left-wing and his cross found King to head in. The referee had blown his whistle though. Callum Wilson had been fouled in the build-up, but worse still, Stanislas was offside when he had received the initial pass from Callum.

On 90 minutes, Bournemouth again looked to have gone ahead when Callum Wilson did an overhead kick that beat Hugo Lloris on his right side. While the players went off to celebrate, VAR took another look at the goal and the ball glanced Josh King's arm. The three points were taken away there and then. We were back at 0-0.

As Adam Smith's injury had stopped the game for a long time, there were 12 minutes of added time, still time to win the game.

Indeed, Bournemouth created a great chance. Callum Wilson made a cross-field ball to Harry Wilson, who was in the clear with just Lloris to beat. But the winger could only shoot right at the keeper. The chance had gone. Bournemouth had to settle for a clean sheet and a point.

This was the only point that Bournemouth had gained since the restart. It was the first bit of momentum in the right direction. While the Cherries could have won the game, they had also been let off a penalty decision in the first half. So, settling for a point was good enough for Eddie Howe. 'We are still in the fight,' he said.

Callum Wilson's denied goal by VAR was hard to get out of the system, even for Eddie Howe. 'That's the beauty of VAR, or not, unfortunately, for us, 'he said. 'It looked, when Callum hit it, like it was a good goal, but you are waiting and there's a lull in proceedings, you fear the worst and yes, it's hit Josh King's arm.'

As fans, we hadn't known if the players were really fighting now or had been paralysed before. But the Spurs performance was a good one. If there could have been a good draw, when you really need to win, then this game was it. But for a loose arm from Josh King, the Cherries could have been celebrating three points, but that's football.

Injury-wise Bournemouth also lost Adam Smith for the next match with his concussion and David Brooks was clearly struggling. The positives were that Bournemouth managed nine shots against Spurs with two on target. The bad vibes were that the team was still finding goals hard to come by.

While Bournemouth fans could feel a little happier about their team, the Saturday results of West Ham United and Watford soon brought us back down to earth. They both won and opened up a six-point gap on Bournemouth. Before the Cherries played Leicester, Aston Villa also won against Crystal Palace and Bournemouth sunk to 19th in the table.

Suddenly, the Leicester City match did feel like a must-win game. Eddie Howe made three changes to the line-up with Arnaut Danjuma, Dominic Solanke and Jack Stacey making the starting line-up, while Josh King missed out with a hamstring problem. Junior Stanislas and Adam Smith also had to sit it out with the latter having suffered a concussion in the Spurs match.

Bournemouth would be most worried about Jamie Vardy, who was leading the chase for the Golden Boot. Sure enough, Vardy would score his 23rd goal of the season in the 23rd minute of the game to put Leicester City 0-1 up. The goal came about after Dan Gosling had lost the ball on halfway. Kelechi Iheanacho put in a cross to the six-yard box that Lloyd Kelly made a poor attempt at, trying to clear with a backheel and Vardy pounced to score. It was a horrible goal and the players knew it, because there had been mistakes made all the way through it.

The match was going Leicester's way and there didn't look like any encouragement for Bournemouth. Nathan Aké had to make a block on a Jamie Vardy shot on 39 minutes. The block only came around because Danjuma had put in a back pass, without looking, straight to Vardy. We didn't know at the time, but Aké's challenge would put him out for the rest of the season, even though he was on the bench for the last game against Everton.

Eddie Howe had to make changes and he did at half-time. While Steve Cook had already come on for the injured Nathan Aké, he also brought on Philip Billing and Junior Stanislas. Off went Dan Gosling who had a poor game and Arnaut Danjuma, who just hadn't been up for the challenge.

The difference in the second half was massive. It still needed a stroke of luck to get a start and Kasper Schmeichel helped out when he hit a goal kick right at Wilfred Ndidi's backside. Callum Wilson got to the ball first and was tripped by Ndidi in the box when Schmeichel was coming out. A penalty was awarded and Junior Stanislas stepped up to score, putting the ball down the middle of the goal on 66 minutes.

A second goal soon followed when Solanke took a high ball down the left-wing and only had eyes for the goal. He took on Schmeichel and slipped the ball underneath the keeper to make it 2-1 on 67 minutes. While Callum Wilson went to pick the ball out of the net and ran into Söyünco, the Turkish defender kicked Wilson back and was immediately given a red card. Leicester went down to 10-men.

Bournemouth played with confidence now. Stanislas was running the show and he popped up on 83 minutes with a couple of stepovers and a shot that deflected in off Jonny Evans to make it 3-1.

Now we were watching the goal difference and

# NO WAY BACK?

hoping Bournemouth could score more to close up the goal difference between them and Watford. Dominic Solanke suddenly started to sparkle. He intercepted a Leicester pass and rounded a defender with a delightful shimmy, before nutmegging Schmeichel and grabbing his second and Bournemouth's fourth goal of the night.

Bournemouth hadn't come back to win a game like this since August 2018. Solanke who had scored no goals in 38 attempts now had two goals in one game. Bournemouth had shocked the football world again.

Before the game ended, we saw Sam Surridge come on and hit the bar in injury time and Leicester's Harvey Barnes forced a late save from Aaron Ramsdale. The 4-1 win couldn't have come at a more important time and Bournemouth fans could now wonder whether their team could fight their way out of trouble again.

The smile on Eddie Howe's face was very wide. 'We came out in the second half with a different mentality really,' he said. 'And I think we played very well in that second period and I'm delighted for the players.

'At half-time it looked pretty bleak for us. We hadn't played well. Leicester had played well and was the better team. There's no denying that. But we responded really well in that second half and that is when your character is truly examined when you are against it the most. The players responded and showed we still had some fight left in us.'

'We had to win tonight. There is hope. We are still in there and we won't stop until the last ball of this season is kicked. We are still up against it. It's still very difficult but I still believe we have the players that can get the results that we need. I have always believed that all the way through,' added Eddie.

Bournemouth fans suddenly had something to smile about since the restart and with that vital win gained, we looked forward to an even bigger challenge – Man City.

Before the match against Man City, I spoke with Dan of the *One Football blog* and was surprised that he thought Bournemouth had a chance of getting something at the Etihad, after the fight they had shown against Leicester City.

I asked these questions before Bournemouth played Man City and I wasn't too optimistic that Bournemouth would pass much more than the 31 points mark, which is what they were on.

CC: Are you surprised Bournemouth are in trouble?

OF: A little bit yes, because you seemed to have established yourselves as a pretty comfortable lower mid-table club and I would have backed you to stay up pretty easily before the season began.

# NO WAY BACK?

I must admit I haven't watched a great deal of Bournemouth this season, but I did see the recent Newcastle defeat and I was pretty alarmed by your performance that night.

Before the win over Leicester, I wouldn't have given you much hope of survival, but now you never know.

CC: Is there any hope for Bournemouth?

OF: Given City play Arsenal in the FA Cup semi-final on Saturday, I think there's a good chance of Guardiola resting players for the Bournemouth game, so there's some hope for you there.
The fact it's also a massive game in terms of Bournemouth's survival hopes but a dead rubber for City could give your boys the edge too. I'm not saying I'm expecting us to lose, but I wouldn't be hugely surprised if we did.

CC: Wow, a Man City fan who thinks they can slip-up against lowly Bournemouth. Thanks, Dan. I'll take any hope you can provide in what has been a desperate position for AFC Bournemouth. I suppose even a weakened Man City team will have players trying to prove a point to the manager though. I think that could be the danger in this game. Man City are a good team whoever they put out and it is all for Bournemouth to do. Still, being the underdog has never shaken Bournemouth and they'll try and rise to this game like it was a final.

The press conference ahead of the Man City game saw Eddie Howe in a little more cheerful mood than he had been for the previous few weeks. 'Winning is everything,' said Eddie Howe when referring to the win over Leicester. 'Winning breeds so many good and positive outcomes from it which is absolutely what we needed. And you can see a lift in the players. A bounce in their step. Renewed confidence. New belief and we now go into three games that we have left with a very positive mindset.'

Preparing for Man City is a very different game to any other. Eddie Howe knew he had to try and elevate the team to levels had not produced so far in the season. But the injuries were growing. Nathan Aké was out, while Adam Smith, Chris Mepham and Simon Francis were all not available for selection.

In the end, Eddie Howe made four changes. There were starts for Steve Cook, Josh King, Philip Billing and Junior Stanislas. So, Callum Wilson and David Brooks were left on the bench.

The game started pretty much as was expected. Man City took the lead on six minutes after Lerma had given a foul away on the edge of Bournemouth's box. David Silva just composed himself before striking the ball in off the bar, and right in the top corner to evade the dive of Aaron Ramsdale.

It was going to be hard to keep the goals down

and Man City hadn't even started with the star names of Kevin de Bruyne, Raheem Sterling, or Riyad Marhez. They were keen to put the game to bed early though. Bournemouth managed to get a free kick of their own and when Junior Stanislas hit it, the ball looked to be bending in until Ederson's dive pushed it on to the post and safety. Solanke also went close but was blocked in the six-yard box. Any hopes of a Bournemouth revival were dashed when Jesus jigged his way past Jack Stacey and Steve Cook, before scoring past Ramsdale on 39 minutes.

Lerma almost gave a penalty away for blocking off Jesus from the ball, but VAR went with Bournemouth on this occasion.

Bournemouth thought they had a goal back in the 60$^{th}$ minute when King finished off a cross from Stanislas at the far post. VAR was called in and John Stones had done just enough to make King offside.

Steve Cook was the next suspect for a penalty when he challenged Jesus, but VAR reversed referee Lee Mason's penalty decision. Bournemouth started to bring on substitutes, as they knew a goal could yet turn the game. Callum Wilson, David Brooks, Lewis Cook and Harry Wilson had all come on in the second half and had added more urgency to Bournemouth's play.

A long throw from Lloyd Kelly caused problems in Man City's box and the ball hit David Silva on the arm, but VAR did not give the penalty. It was a let-off for

City and yet they were coming under more pressure. Bournemouth finally got their reward on 88 minutes when Callum Wilson played David Brooks in and he beat Ederson to score his first goal of the season.

Sam Surridge replaced Billing as Bournemouth went for an added time equaliser. The ball kept bouncing around Man City's box. Callum Wilson had a great chance but drove his shot wide and Sam Surridge almost got on the end of a free kick, while Lewis Cook and Lerma had chances to get the equaliser. It just didn't happen and Bournemouth had to be content with registering 14 shots against Man City, which was the highest of any visiting team to the Etihad in the four years of Guardiola's reign.

However, it was points Bournemouth needed and they had fallen short. 'We gave everything in that match. It was a really good display,' said Eddie Howe. 'Even more so when we went 1-0 down to their first real chance – a quality free kick. We seem to be a victim of those in recent weeks, so that was tough. But we responded well to that and dug in and produced an excellent performance.

'It just didn't bounce right for us in front of goal tonight. Even their second goal is a clinical finish and I think that was probably the difference between the teams,' added Eddie Howe.

While Bournemouth fans could only look on and wonder if their team would get some more points, the government announced that they hoped fans would be back in stadiums by October. There would still have to be some test games first, but getting back to normal was a possibility now.

Moving on to the Southampton game, Bournemouth first received some good news with West Ham beating Watford 3-1 on Friday 17 July. Now Watford lay just three points ahead with a goal difference, just two ahead of the Cherries, with two games to go. Watford had a harder run-in with Man City and Arsenal to play, while West Ham now looked safe on 27 points and a superior goal difference to the teams below them.

Aston Villa was only two goals behind Bournemouth now, having got a point against Everton earlier in the week. Bournemouth fans were just grateful to Theo Walcott who had scored Everton's equaliser in the 87$^{th}$ minute.

The Sunday showdown with Southampton was huge. Bournemouth knew they had to win really to give themselves the best chance of staying up. Eddie Howe let the media know that Adam Smith could make the game, but there was no chance for Nathan Aké, Simon Francis, Charlie Daniels, or Chris Mepham. In came Callum Wilson for Dominic Solanke and David Brooks for Dan Gosling. Southampton made five changes. It didn't affect their rhythm. Southampton got straight on it, winning a corner in the opening minute. While Josh King was struggling to stay on his feet, Danny Ings looked primed to score.

Nathan Redmond would have the first big chance for the Saints, but Ramsdale came out to beat him to the ball. It was the first of many saves he would make.

Although Bournemouth had been winning corners, they couldn't get a shot on target. It was Danny Ings who made space and got a shot off well, just before half-time to give the Saints the first goal.

We hadn't seen enough of David Brooks and he was subbed at half-time. Again, it was Ings threatening to score at the start of the second half, shooting inches wide from the first attack. James Ward-Prowse went closer when his shot was pushed away for a corner. The danger had not passed, though. A handball by Harry Wilson from the corner gifted Danny Ings the chance to make it 0-2. A stuttered run-up led to a shot that Ramsdale read well and saved to his left.

Bournemouth still had hope. The Cherries brought on Lewis Cook and Dominic Solanke for Junior Stanislas and Josh King. Bournemouth had been getting closer with Callum Wilson heading into the side netting.

Eddie Howe was throwing everything at Southampton now with Surridge replacing Lerma. Gosling also came on for Billing and Bournemouth got their chance when Callum Wilson knocked on a ball that fell to Surridge. Surridge finished at the near post on 90 minutes, but VAR ruled it out for Callum Wilson being offside.

It was a bitter blow. A point would have been something, even if not the three-points Bournemouth needed. Another chance saw Harry Wilson and Dan Gosling get in each other's way before Harry Wilson's snapshot was saved by McCarthy for a corner. Instead of equalising, Bournemouth found themselves conceding a second goal, in added time. Michael Obafemi crossed for Ché Adams to score on 90+8 minutes.

It felt like Bournemouth's season was over. Now Watford would just need a point on Tuesday night to relegate Bournemouth and Aston Villa.

Eddie Howe was diplomatic in his verdict of the Southampton defeat. 'I'm devastated, we tried and gave everything. It was a spirited performance, I thought we created chances. It could have gone a very different path today, but the first goal was probably a key moment – we didn't defend well enough and didn't do well at that moment.' said Eddie Howe. 'The second goal, there were seconds left in the game. We kick ourselves. It could have been very different.

'It didn't fall for us in front of goal. That's not the first time it's happened for us this season. But we created the chances today, we just didn't take them. There were a lot of balls in their box and a lot of territory for us and the moments were there – we just didn't take them.'

Eddie Howe wasn't beating himself up too much but was down about how the game slipped away. The mid-week results looked at first to go for Bournemouth with Man City unleashing a 4-0 defeat on Watford to tie-up the goal difference between Watford and Bournemouth at -27, although Watford still had three more points.

However, Arsenal had been flat against Aston Villa and succumbed to a 1-0 away defeat. That put Dean Smith's side three points ahead of Bournemouth and on a goal difference of -26 points with one game to play.

Eddie Howe admitted that he had taken his sons to the golf course on Wednesday when Bournemouth's fate was in the hands of the mid-week results of Aston Villa and Watford. Somehow Eddie had found himself back at home in the hour sitting on the results, hoping for the best.

The calculation was simple. Bournemouth hadn't been relegated yet and would have a chance of staying up on the last day of the season. If Bournemouth won their game against Everton and Aston Villa and Watford lost their games to West Ham United and Arsenal, Bournemouth would stay up on goal difference. If Bournemouth drew or lost to Everton they were down, no matter what happened in the other games. A point for Villa or Watford would also see Bournemouth relegated.

If Bournemouth fans were just getting to grips with all that, what they didn't need to hear from *SkySports* was that Nathan Aké was in talks with Man City over a possible transfer. The price was said to be £35m (later it turned out to be £41m), £5m lower than the first buyback option Chelsea had been said to have on the player, which was believed to have expired in January 2020. Even if Bournemouth were lucky and stayed up, it was hard to see a player of Aké quality turning down such a chance to play under a top coach like Pep Guardiola.

AFC Bournemouth was more concerned in telling fans that they had a new ticketing website, no doubt keen to get everyone thinking about making payments to the club for next season, as soon as the league Bournemouth would be playing in and the dates became known.

The period leading up to the last round of matches on Sunday 26 July was a strange time. In a way, Bournemouth fans felt they had been relegated already, but there was just a glimmer of a chance that a miracle could happen. We'd seen though that Arsenal was not a team you would rely on to play well every game and Aston Villa was a form team taking on West Ham, who had nothing to play for.

Bournemouth stood in 19th place and seemingly least likely to survive. Yet, because there was hope, it was only natural to just want to pray for a win against Everton and to hope that the five-year period in the

Premier League wasn't coming to an end just yet. The reality was that Championship football was more likely next season and, for me at least, it was easier to get used to that thought now, so that it wouldn't be so deflating, when and if, results didn't go our way on the last day of the season.

If Bournemouth fans were left in any doubt of what would happen if they went down, they were soon made clear when Steve Bruce of Newcastle United was reported to be putting together a £25m bid for Callum Wilson.

I wrote about the possibility of Eddie Howe's side being dismantled – it was a tough period. It felt like Bournemouth had been waiting for the final act for a long time. As fans, we just needed to know our fate.

It was the Saturday before the last matches when I received a call from Victoria at *Heart Hampshire and Heart Thames Valley Radio*. She wanted to interview me as an AFC Bournemouth fan, which would be aired the next day before the Everton match.

The weather was so bad that I couldn't get a clear signal to take the call, so I ended up answering Victoria by *Whats App*. The questions and answers went like this.

HR: What would your hopes for tomorrow's game and what worries are you facing at the moment, if Bournemouth ended up being relegated?

CC: 'Tomorrow's game has been building all week

for us fans at Bournemouth. Everton is a team that has been good at home this season and haven't lost at Goodison in the calendar year under Carlo Ancelotti. It's a tough fixture for AFCB. They have to win the game so at least we know what we have to do, but we still have to hope that other results go our way. It's kind of been an anxious period waiting for this and you just hope the players are up for it and really give it everything. Hopefully, we get the win, and then we'll have to wait and see what happens.

'Hopefully, we don't get relegated, but it's been on our minds all season. We haven't had the best of seasons. We haven't won enough games and our defence has been leaking goals consistently, almost two goals a game. We won't be surprised if Bournemouth gets relegated but we hope we get a little bit of a miracle, a little bit of help. We haven't had a lot of luck all season and my main fear I suppose is the financial implications for the club. I think it will be quite severe if we are relegated and there could be quite a few job losses. Certainly, a lot of the players will have to move on, but the fans will still enjoy the Championship as we have not been at that level that often in the past either. The main thing is that we have a football team and that it is still looking to grow and expand. Hopefully, we can still build the academies and new training facility and get back into the Premier League as soon as we can.'

HR: 'What does it mean to you as a Bournemouth fan for the team to be in the Premier League?'

CC: 'It's always been like a dream to get to the Premier League so to have been there for five years has been amazing. We used to sing in the first year that we are only here for one season and it's ended up being a lot longer than that. We have had a good run. We are by far the smallest club in the Premier League in terms of the fanbase and we have probably been pushing above our weight for a little while. Hopefully, we can hang on, and if Eddie Howe manages to pull it off this season I think the club will only get stronger.'

HR: What has it been like for you as a fan during lockdown and how will you be showing your support tomorrow – celebrating at home?

CC: Lockdown has been hard working from home. But as a fan of the football club it has been interesting. I haven't enjoyed the matches as much without the atmosphere and routine. I am a fan who lives in Surrey, so I have to travel down to Bournemouth every home game and away games require travel as well. It's not been as good. Tomorrow, season ticket holders have been given a *NowTV* pass to watch the game from the club so that was kind of them. I'll be watching with my two sons and we'll try not to get too nervous but it's going to be very exciting.'

Eddie Howe's pre-match interview still proved that he had hope. The Championship end of season games with Barnsley escaping relegation and Swansea needing a six-goal swing to make the play-offs showed why everyone just loves the game, he added. Bournemouth might have to prepare themselves for similar swings in emotion, but his players would have to simply concentrate on trying to win the game against Everton. If they couldn't win the game they'd be down anyway. Eddie mentioned that there is a belief that we can win our game, but that is easier said than done.

'Win our game and then who knows, that's the unpredictability of football,' said Eddie. 'You are hoping we get a bit of luck.'

Adam Smith would be in contention to start and there would be a late call on Nathan Aké, who had a groin strain.

Eddie Howe made three changes for the game. Adam Smith would start along with Dominic Solanke and Dan Gosling, as Bournemouth went looking for goals. Nathan Aké made it onto the bench and was joined by Philip Billing and Junior Stanislas who had started the previous game.

Bournemouth started impressively, chasing down every Everton player. Possession soon settled with Bournemouth and Callum Wilson was prevented from putting the Cherries ahead by a spectacular one-handed save by Jordan Pickford.

Eddie Howe didn't have to wait long though to see his side take the lead. Josh King was fouled by Jarrard Branthwaite on the edge of the box on 10 minutes. David Brooks took the free kick that deflected up off the wall and towards Callum Wilson. Wilson headed it on and the ball touched Richarlison's arm before King could get to it and Solanke turned to shoot, only for Pickford to save. Referee Chris Kavanagh spotted Richarlison's handball and gave the penalty. Josh King then stepped up to score his seventh goal of the season and put Bournemouth ahead on 13 minutes, despite Pickford guessing the right way.

A couple of minutes later it looked like Bournemouth had a good shout for another penalty. David Brooks was in the box with Lucas Digne when the ball clearly hit Digne's arm, but VAR did not rule it as an infringement.

Bournemouth were also making some good blocks with Kelly playing particularly well to keep stopping Richarlison's shots. Theo Walcott did get through on goal, but Ramsdale stood tall to make a sharp save. By this time, Bournemouth fans knew Watford were losing 2-0 to Arsenal, and West Ham were still drawing 0-0 with Aston Villa.

Meanwhile, at Goodison, Everton came more and more into the game. Bournemouth fans could at least relax about the score at the Emirates which went to 3-0 in Arsenal's favour.

Everton hadn't given up though and with Coleman's run past Rico, Bournemouth soon had problems. Walcott was played in down the side and pulled the ball back across the six-yard line for Moise Kean to tap home on 42 minutes. That would see Bournemouth relegated, if they couldn't score again.

As if the nerves weren't enough, Watford grabbed a goal back at Arsenal 3-1.

Bournemouth fans could breathe again when Solanke won a free kick on the left-wing. Rico played a high cross into the box and Solanke rose well ahead of Lerma, to score with a header. It was his third league goal of the season. Bournemouth led 1-2 at half-time.

With Watford 3-1 down at Arsenal and West Ham being held 0-0 by Aston Villa Bournemouth just needed West Ham to score to be safe.

The second half was going to decide matters in these three games. Everton came out trying to force the pace with an early corner. Ramsdale stood firm and caught the ball, before a long kick saw Callum Wilson try and blast a shot past Pickford form the edge of the box. Pickford had to make a good save from Wilson's shot.

While Everton made changes, Bournemouth found themselves under some pressure. Lloyd Kelly brushed the ball with his arm, but no penalty was awarded. Solanke then raced back to make a great tackle on Richarlison.

Bournemouth subbed Solanke and Brooks to bring on Billing and Stanislas on 64 minutes. Eddie Howe was probably looking to defend more in numbers with five in midfield. The score from Watford's game didn't engender confidence, as the Hornets had brought the score back to 3-2. Another goal for Watford and Bournemouth could expect relegation.

While Ancelotti was pressing harder for a goal by bringing on Dominic Calvert-Lewin, the Stanislas substitution was about to pay off for Bournemouth. Following a corner, he had his back to goal and was heading towards his half, chased by Anthony Gordon. But Stanislas was biding his time, turned sharply, and played a one-two with Rico. Stanislas was away, driving at goal and kept Anthony Gordon and Michael Keane at bay before stroking the ball past Pickford and into the far corner. Bournemouth were 1-3 up on 80 minutes.

The Cherries were on their way to their first away win of 2020. They had done their job. It was all about whether the scores would change in the other games. Then we heard that Jack Grealish had scored for Aston Villa. It was the worst news possible. West Ham would need to score two goals in the last six minutes of their game to save Bournemouth from relegation.

Crazy as it seemed, a deflected shot from Yarmolenko saw West Ham pull the score back to 1-1 against Aston Villa. With Watford still losing 3-2 to Arsenal, Bournemouth just needed West Ham to score once more. It was an agonising wait when Bournemouth's game finished 1-3. Eddie Howe knew the scores as they kept being flashed up on the big scoreboard at Goodison. Then the final whistle went at the London Stadium. Aston Villa had got a 1-1 draw. Bournemouth were automatically relegated.

Watford was still playing at Arsenal but couldn't get the two goals they needed to overhaul Aston Villa and would end a place below Bournemouth in 19th.

Aston Villa was safe on 35 points, just a point ahead of Bournemouth. Bournemouth had climbed above Watford on goal difference on -25 goals compared to -28, but 34 points saw both teams go down with only Norwich City below them on 21 points.

'It's an incredibly difficult moment for us,' said Eddie Howe. 'We always felt we were capable of a last-minute escape. All the way through the game today, I didn't know the scores were going to be on the scoreboard, so we sort of had that teased in our face. But the lads put it to the back of their heads and played well today. I was very pleased with the performance. It was the best we have played in a long, long time. We showed the ability has always been there.'

'Ultimately, you have to look back at the season and all the points we have not got which we should have done and every team will feel the same way. But it's such small margins in the end that we have gone down on. It's incredibly painful when you look back. We have dipped below the levels we were at in previous seasons. There is no denying that and as manager, I have to take the ultimate responsibility for that. I'm just incredibly disappointed for the club and the fans, who aren't able to be here, who have always been so good with me and the team. I feel desperately sorry for them today. Our supporters have always been brilliant for us, home and away.

Asked whether the fans would have made a difference if they could have been at Bournemouth's games after the restart, Eddie Howe had this to say. 'They have made a difference for us down the years. There is no denying that. When we have been dead and buried in games, they are the ones that have got a little bit more out of the team and we have managed to pull off some great results. So, we missed them [the fans] certainly in the early lockdown games. We certainly did, we took a while to get going after lockdown and that slow start ultimately I think has probably cost us.'

While Eddie Howe was considering where it had gone wrong, and if he should look to carry on, AFC Bournemouth came out with a suggestion that they could make a legal challenge on Hawk-Eye's failure in the Sheffield United v Aston Villa game at the start of project restart, when Villa's keeper took the ball over the goal line, but referee Michael Oliver and Hawk-Eye failed to award the goal. The point that Villa gained that day enabled them to stay up at Bournemouth's expense.

I hoped that Bournemouth would just accept the league table as it was. 'The world of sport is a pretty unsavoury place. We know the Premier League is ruled by money, and for a club like Bournemouth to fall out of it, when 85 per cent of its outgoings go on player salaries, is going to be a catastrophe. But there is honour in the game and sportsmanship which are much better values to uphold, and if Bournemouth did launch a compensation claim, it would reek of sour grapes, rather than a valid claim to seek justice, 'I wrote on *Cherry Chimes*.

Bournemouth needed leadership in this moment of crisis and it came from the owner Maxim Demin, who is usually fairly anonymous. But he made a statement that grabbed everyone's attention. He underlined that he was committed to taking the club back to the Premier League, that some of our young players could thrive in the Championship and that unity would get the club through this difficult period.

While we tried to digest his words to feel better about the situation, it was left to the club to move things forward by sending out details of how fans could renew their season tickets. Even the 2020-21 season was likely to be strange as a ballot system would be introduced to give everyone a chance of attending any reduced capacity games. Somehow, football had changed.

For myself, the news that my eldest son Robert had gained a place at Bath University to study film, TV and digital production and knowing that my younger son, Stephen, needed to earn money at weekends, meant the end of our family trips to Dean Court. Things hadn't been helped by myself having to take a pay-cut, because of the impact of coronavirus on the publishing company I work for. Going to football games would be a luxury, so things had to change.

Seeing AFC Bournemouth play for more than the last decade has been a terrific period of my life. if I still lived in Bournemouth, I would probably continue to go to matches even on my own. But now it is time for me to sit back and spend more time with my family. However, I'll always have one eye on the scoreboard of AFC Bournemouth and may still attend the odd match when I can.

When it was announced on 1 August 2020 that Eddie Howe had left the club by mutual consent, I knew for sure then that something had broken at AFCB and it would need time to heal.

It's the end of an era, but I wouldn't have missed it for the world. UTCIAD!

# Chapter 14. – Player Index

Nathan Aké 10-11, 20, 22, 28-29, 56-57, 62, 64, 92, 95, 106, 109, **117-119**, 124, **141-144**, 149, 156, 158, 164, 170, 172, 176, 180, 187-188, 204, 231, 238, 251-252, 256, 259, 263, 267
Harry Arter 20, **22-23**
Jaidon Anthony 22
Artur Boruc 4, 19, 27-28, 31, 85, 195, 199, 234, 245
Asmir Begović 3-4, 12, 26, **49**, 52, 140, **144**, 196
Neill Blake 171, 197, 201
Philip Billing 22-23, 27-29, 32-33, 36-38, 45, 57, 62, 64, 80-81, 92, 106, 114, 125, 128, 133, 139-140, 144, 147-148, 153, **158**, **164-165**, 173-176, 187-189, 198, 204, 206, 230, 232, 234, 237-238, 244, 252, 256, 258, 260, 267, 270
David Brooks **21-24**, 30, 35, 39, 70, 83, 104, 116, 152, 168, 180, 189, 202, **215**, 226, 230, 234, 238, 241-242, 249-250, 256-260, 268, 270
Matt Butcher 21, 26, 156

Lewis Cook 22, 24, 50, **52-53**, 56, 64, 74, 77, 80-81, 92, 95, 109, 117, 120, 130, 133-134, 144, 154, 165, 174, 176, 188, 230, 237-238, 244, 246, 257-258, 260

Steve Cook **27-29**, 46, 52, 57, 62, 64, 81-82, 92, 106, 114, 124, 127-129, 134, 143, **148**, 157, 162-163, 169, 172, 174, 187, 189, 195, 204, 226, 230, 233-234, 239, 244, 247, 252, 256-257

Nathaniel Clyne 8

Tyler Cordner 22

Harry Cornick 139

Charlie Daniels 24, 26, 31, **37**, **39**, 51, 71, 143, 180, **199**, 234, 259

Arnaut Danjuma **24**, 27-28, 33, 61, 69, 73-74, 77, 79, 81-83, 85, 106, 109, 118, 123, 180, 189, 202, 231, 233-234, 237, 246, 249, 251-252

Will Dennis 22, 26, 28

Sylvain Distin 88

Jermain Defoe **153**, 234

Alex Dobre 26, 28

Dickie Dowsett **204**

Carl Fletcher 97, 104

Steve Fletcher 21, **160**

Simon Francis 8, 24, 28, 50, 73-74, **105**, 107, 110, 115-116, 120, 124-125, 128, 133-135, 143-144, 148, 157-159, 162-164, 172-174, 199, 202, 234, 256, 259

Ryan Fraser 5, 18, 20, 26, 30, 39, 45, 52, 56, 70, 77-79, 85, 89, 92, **95-96**, **104**, 114-115, 118, 120-121, 125, 130, 133, 135, 139, 148, 156-158, 164, 169-170, 174, 185, 188, 199, **228**, 230, 234, 242

PLAYER INDEX 277

Jimmy Glass 115
Dan Gosling 18, 95, 117, 120-**121**, 128, 144, 157-158, 163-165, 171, 174, 176, 188, 232, 238, 248, 251-252, 259-261, 267
Eddie Howe V, XV, 2-5, 10, 12-16, 19-20, 22, 25, 27-29, 31-32, **34-36, 38-44**, 46-47, 49-51, 53, 55-56, 58-59, 61, 69-72, 74, 76-78, 82-85, 90, 94-95, 98, **100-101**, 104-106, 108, 114, 116-120, 122-130, 134, 136-141, **143-147,** 149-155, 157, 159, 163, 165, 167-168, 170, 174-177, 181, 189, 191, 195-196, 201, 203, 215, 229-231, 233-234, 237-239, 242, 244-246, 250-253, 256, 258-262, 264, 266-268, 270-272, 274
Richard Hughes 201
Jordan Ibe 1, 20-22, 26, 30, 36, 45, **97**, 118, 141-143, 159, **179**, 199, 234, 250
Danny Ings 259, 260
Corey Jordan 26, 28
Lloyd Kelly **2**, 23-24, 31, 39, 61, 127, 143, 150, 153, 198, 233, **237**, 244, 246-247, 249, 251, 257, 268-279
Josh King 27-28, 34, 36, 38, 45, 52-54, 56-57, 62, 64-66, 73, 77, 79, 81, 83, 85, **89**, 92, 95-96, 102-103, 105, 109, **119-121**,128, 130-131, 1Lalana
47, 150, **155**, **168-169**, 171-172, 176, 180, 185, 187, 189, 194, 230-232, 237, 241, 246, 248-251, 256-257, 259-260, **268**
Jefferson Lerma 1, 22-23, 25-26, 29, 37, 45, 56, 64, 77, 80-82, 89, 95, 102-104, 106, 114, 121, 130, 133-134, 144, **159**, **163-165**, 169, 172, 176, 187-188, 230, 238, 248, 256-258, 260, 269

Connor Mahoney 9
Chris Mepham 21, 26, 29, 31, 34, 37, 42, 45-46, 52, 102, 114, 1117, 120, 124, 130, **143**, 150, 180, 202, 244, 247, 256, 259
Tyrone Mings 6, 36, 198
Neil Moss 171, 179
Lys Mousset 18-19, 138, 167-168, 170, 180, 198
Nnamdi Ofoborh 20, 26-28
Brett Pitman 169, 204
Marc Pugh 14, 104, 202, 229
Aaron Ramsdale 4, 17-20, 27-28, **33-35**, 37, 42, 46, 49, 51, 53, 57, 64, 66, 73, 75, 78, 81, 85, 89, 91-92, 95-96, 102, 108, 120, **124**, 128-130, 134-135, 144, 148-149, 151-152, 158-159, 161, 165-166, 170, 172-173, 175, 177, 182, 185-186, 188, 222, 230, 238, 245-246, 253, 256-257, 260, 268-269
Jamie Redknapp 220
Harry Redknapp V, 186
Diego Rico 22, 28, 31, 33, 37, 39, 42-43, 51-52, 64, 71, 73, **78-80**, 82-83, 91, 127-129, 134, 143, 147, 150-151, 157, 172, 228, 244, 269-270
Matt Ritchie 13, 61, 94, 219
Sam Sherring 22, 26, 28
Jack Simpson 20, 26, 49, 123, 134, 149, **160-161**, 193-194
Dominic Solanke 21-22, 25-26, 45, 52, 54-56, 64, 73, 78, 80-81, 85, 109, 114, 121, 126, 130, 135, 137, **139-140**, 142, 150, 174, 180, 188, 198, 233, 237, 245, 247, **251-253**, 257, 259-260, **267-270**

PLAYER INDEX

Adam Smith 8, 24, 28, 31-32, 47, 51-52, 62, 69, 77, 83, 85, 89, 92, 95, 109, 114, 116, 143-144, 157, 162,167, **173**, 219, 230-232, 238, 244-245, 145, **248-151**, 256, 259, 267

Brad Smith 69, 140, 142-143, 234

Nigel Spackman 103

Jack Stacey **16**, 21, 24-26, 31-32, 33, 37,45, 51-52, 55, 57, 61, 64, **66**, 74, 77, 109, 120, 128, 131, 143, 147, 150, 169, 172, 175-176, 185, 198, 230, 233, 237, 248, 251, 257

Junior Stanislas 50, 70, 120, 123, 126, 130, 133, 135, 140, 169-170, 174, 176, 187-188, 219, 232, 234, 237, **244-245**, 248-249, **251-252**, 256-257, 260, 267, **270**

Andrew Surman 26, 29, 32, 49, 143, 165, 169, 174, 234

Sam Surridge 21-22, 26, 28, 138, **154**, 253, 258, 260

Kyle Taylor 140

Jason Tindall 14, 72, 74, 83, 201

Mark Travers 2-3, 5, 19-21, 25-26, 45, 49, 51, 59, 139-140, **144**, 153, 245

Callum Wilson 9, 16-18, 27, 36, 46, **52-54**, 57-58, 62, 64-65, 70, 73, 78, 82, 85, 92, 95, 106, 110, 114-115, 117, 119, 126-130, 133, 137, 140, 147-148, 150-151, 157, 159, 170, 172-173, 176, 185, 187, 223, 230, 232-233, 237, **248-249**, 252, 256, 258-261, 267, 269

Harry Wilson **7**, 24, **29-31,** 33, 35-37, 39-40, 42-45, 52, 54-57, 62, 64, 69-70, 75, 79, 81-83, 92, 95, 97, 102, 106, 109-110, 114, 118, 123, 128-129, **134**, 139-140, 144, 148, 150, 152, 157-158, 169, **173-174**, 182, 187,

199, 215, 226, 228, 230, 232-233, 248-249, 257, **260-261**
Jordan Zemura 26, 28

Printed in Great Britain
by Amazon